CHANGE
YOUR
VOICE
CHANGE
YOUR
LIFE

CHANGE YOUR VOICE

CHANGE YOUR LIFE

A Quick, Simple Plan for
Finding and Using Your
Natural, Dynamic Voice

DR. MORTON COOPER

Voice & Speech Company of America
Los Angeles

Hardcover edition published by Macmillan Publishing Co. 1984

First HarperPerennial edition published 1985.

Voice and Speech Company of America, 17th printing, 1999.

Library of Congress Cataloging in Publication Data

Cooper, Morton, 1931—
    Change your voice, change your life.

    (Everyday handbook)
    Reprint. Originally published: New York: Macmillan, 1984.
    1. Voice culture. I. Title
PN4162.C65   1985   808.5   84-48589
ISBN 0-87980-441-6   (pbk)

To my mother, Mae, who encouraged me to be everything I could be, and to my wife, Marcia, and daughters, Lorna and Marla, who let me, and to my father, Louis, who died when I was eight, for the legacy of love and kindness he gave me

Contents

PART TWO
Sound and (Voice) Suicide

Acknowledgments

While it has long been my ambition to write a book for the general public on the benefits of healthy voice usage and effective voice sound, this dream could only have been realized with the support and guidance of many individuals to whom I shall be forever grateful. Unfortunately, space limitations preclude my mentioning them all. There are a special few, however, whom I would like to formally acknowledge for their part in bringing this book to fruition.

My wife, Marcia Ann Hartung Cooper, deserves first mention, both for her loving personal encouragement, and her significant professional contribution to my work.

Kathy Robbins demonstrated remarkable agenting skills in finding a home for a thesis on an unheard of subject. In addition, she provided focus and invaluable structuring suggestions in the developmental stages of writing.

Hillel Black, publisher of Macmillan Publishing Company, allowed my dream to become a reality by inviting me to proceed with my efforts to educate readers on this critical subject. I am deeply indebted to him for his commitment to this endeavor and also for his kind and expert words of advice. Associate editor Dominick Anfuso lent polish and grace to the final draft.

But the writing of this book could not have been accomplished without the assistance of Leslie Bart, who gave a literary voice to both my practical voice and my methods of treatment.

Heartfelt thanks, too, to the many laryngologists and

medical doctors who have recognized the value of my therapy as well as the importance of healthy voice techniques. Though I cannot mention all who have endorsed my findings, I take this opportunity to express my appreciation to Henry J. Rubin, M.D., associate professor of the Department of Head and Neck Surgery at the UCLA School of Medicine; and the late Joel J. Pressman, M.D., former Chairman of the Head and Neck Division at the UCLA Medical Center.

Professional colleagues to whom I am long-indebted for their help and support are: Virgil Anderson, Ph.D., former Director of the Speech Pathology Division at Stanford University; and Elise Hahn, Ph.D., former Director of the Speech Pathology Division at UCLA.

And the more recent support of the Mayo Clinic and other esteemed medical institutions is also manifestly appreciated.

I thank Andrea Burke for her secretarial assistance in the formulation of this book; and my brother, Everett Cooper, for his trust and confidence in me.

Lastly and most importantly, I would like to express my deepest gratitude to my patients who permitted me to tell their personal stories. Though their names, and in most cases their occupations and hometowns, have been altered to protect their privacy, their problems and experiences most graphically illustrate the need for greater public awareness on the correct use of the speaking voice. The public figures and celebrities who have generously allowed me to use their real names in reference to their therapy are owed a particular debt. Their place in society presents them as role models and so their examples are enormously helpful in reaching the public with my important message.

MORTON COOPER, PH.D.

CHANGE
YOUR
VOICE
CHANGE
YOUR
LIFE

PART ONE

Success
and
Sound

1

The Secret of Success

THE MAGIC

Some people have the magic. They are seductive but not weak. They are controlling but not aggressive. They are filled, quite simply, with an intangible power that commands attention and generates success.

Franklin Delano Roosevelt, thirty-second president of the United States, had the magic. So did Sir Winston Churchill, British prime minister from 1940 to 1945. Each was possessed of that rare ability to convince others of his way of seeing the world, his way of saving the world.

Today, Roosevelt is remembered by Americans—Democrats and Republicans alike—as a leader of unprecedented magnetism. Churchill remains Great Britain's most esteemed statesman. The preeminence of each man is intact, decades after he made his mark on the world.

There is, of course, a lesson to be learned from the successes of these leaders. There is an example to be drawn from them. And that is to identify the source of the intangible power that advances people such as Roosevelt and Churchill above and beyond others with similar aspirations and potentially equal talents. And the logical next step is to tap into their magic, the magic that gave *them* the edge on greatness.

That is the purpose of this book: To demonstrate that the one trait shared by almost all who achieve greatness is the power of communication, and to show you how to acquire that power and incorporate it into your own life.

You may be surprised to discover that successful communication depends largely on effective use of the voice. What may surprise you even more is that, with a little bit of self-awareness and the application of practical principles, a magical voice of success can be yours.

I am referring here to what I call a "right" voice, one that is well produced and natural and healthy. Such a voice is a valuable asset. It can have, quite literally, a hypnotic and powerful hold on your listeners.

By contrast, an inefficient or unpleasant or misplaced sound has a detrimental effect. A voice imbued with negative symptoms or traits will hurt rather than help. It will inhibit rather than enhance. It is a "wrong" voice.

There are exceptions to this rule, as you'll see later in this chapter. But while some people have managed to turn deficient or improperly produced voices to advantage, there is one law that holds fast: The manner in which you express yourself is the key to your identity.

If you doubt this simple truth, consider the extent to which you judge others by their vocal presentation.

Reflect, if you will, on the people who have made life's most lasting impressions on you, good and bad. A teacher, perhaps. A parent. An authority. A colleague. A competitor. Any role model from any epoch of your life.

Do you remember their attire? Their posture? The color of their eyes? The shape of their ears? The style of their hair? It's strange how those visual perceptions fade over time, but they do. In most instances, what remains is a *voice image*.

Though voice image is probably a new concept to you, it is one of the most vital, pervasive, meaningful, and controlling factors in your life. It pertains to sound and persona. It designates the way you perceive your own sound and the way you perceive others' sounds, as well as the interpretive judgments you apply to those sounds.

These judgments constitute a qualitative response. They please or displease you. They engage you or repel you. All too often, they just leave you indifferent. But in any case, it is the positive or negative value that you place on these sounds that lingers, and thus determines not only your immediate impression of another, but your long-lasting recollection of that person.

How often have you said of an acquaintance or colleague: "He's a great guy, but he'd be a lot easier to take if he didn't whine on about things. He makes me uncomfortable . . ."?

This suggests a negative voice image is at work. A wrong voice can cause an individual to be viewed and remembered as an unattractive person.

Conversely, you have without doubt met another whose effect on you was inexplicably positive: "I was prepared to dislike her. In fact, I was dreading meeting her. But she won me over. I don't know what it was about her, but I was taken with everything she said."

Some people call this charisma. Others call it presence. I call it a positive and compelling voice image, a voice that draws you into its spell. Such a voice presents the substance and character of the speaker, as well as the content of his ideas, in a positive light.

This is why I say that your manner of expression— and by this I refer to *how* you use your voice—is the key to your identity.

THE WINNING COMPONENT IS HOW . . .

In short, others may not listen to *what* you say—and may not have a flattering impression of *who* you are—unless they are engaged by *how you say it.*

My aim is to teach you how to say it—anything and everything you wish to convey to the world—in a manner that will enhance your personal and professional life, as well as your physical well-being.

Yes, the way you use your voice does affect your health. What no one has ever told you before is that incorrect voice usage—amounting to misuse and abuse of the vocal mechanism—can not only hinder your relations with the world, but can physically harm you.

The physical consequences of voice abuse (leading to *voice suicide!*), will be covered fully in Part Two of this book. So, too, will special problems such as stuttering and dysphasia.

My methods for achieving healthy voice technique evolved over many years, beginning with my early studies at Brooklyn College and at Indiana University, and continuing through an assistantship at Stanford University, a Ph.D. program at UCLA, a period as Director of the Voice and Speech Clinic, Head and Neck Surgery Division at UCLA School of Medicine, and twenty years in private practice.

Throughout my career in the field of vocal rehabilitation, my work has focused primarily on the treatment of voice pathology. I have encountered and treated almost every imaginable type of voice disorder. What I have learned in the process is that most voice disorders could have been prevented by the correct use of the vocal mechanism. And furthermore, it has become increasingly apparent that the vast majority of Americans —those with *and* without obvious impairment of the voice—know little, if anything, about how to properly use their own voices.

This helps explain why so few people in our society have "the magic"—the magic of a Roosevelt or a Churchill.

Churchill, by the way, was not born to eloquent speech, as you might have imagined. In fact, he was terribly hampered in his early years by a stutter. Hardly an auspicious beginning for a politician who would go on to become a great orator.

And yet he moved many to tears in 1940 when he intoned dramatically before the House of Commons: "Never in the field of human conflict was so much owed by so many to so few."

These beautifully enunciated words were spoken in tribute to those in the Royal Air Force who had died fighting for their country. Imagine the same sentence delivered with a stutter. Its impact would have been, to put it kindly, greatly reduced.

But Churchill had by now overcome his deficiency. He had mastered the elements of voice production. He spoke with resounding resonance. His rate of speech was excellent. And his control of volume was arresting. He had the magic, and he used it to his advantage.

I cannot emphasize strongly enough or often enough that these tools for successful communication can be readily acquired by you. They are simple to learn and demand only some time and self-awareness.

Call the process voice retraining, if you like. Or think of it as a course in self-improvement. Labels are not important. It's the reward that matters.

The obvious reward of achieving correct voice production is that it enables you to realize the full potential of *your* natural voice. In other words, to make yours the voice of success.

By this, I mean a voice that properly and advantageously represents YOU. It should be both pleasant to listen to and comfortable to use. It should attract, not alienate, your listeners. It shouldn't crack or break and mustn't require constant throat clearing (which may well be a sign of pathology). Yours can and should be a natural voice that guarantees your being heard because others are captivated by the sound you make.

LET'S LOOK AT WHERE YOU WENT WRONG

Perhaps you consider this a formidable task? You've heard your voice on a tape recorder and you already know that your "normal" sound is too nasal, too weak, too high, or too raspy. It whines or it barks. Or else, it simply doesn't work half the time.

Or, worse, maybe you have tried to change your voice in an attempt to assume a *voice image* that appeals to you. You thus play games with your voice, forcing it to highs or lows that you believe will add authority or sensuality, intelligence or charm, to your presence.

If so, you have probably usurped a voice that is not physically natural to your own vocal apparatus. You have effectively aggravated existent bad voice habits by adding new ones.

And for those of you who have persisted with tones forced from the lower throat, you've managed to achieve hoarseness or a loss of volume. Your friends and colleagues have ceased listening to you. Either they can't understand you or they can't hear you. A few of you may already have had nodes or polyps surgically removed because of prolonged use of this disastrous voice pattern.

And that is what *all* voices are: patterns. Habits, actually. In all too many instances, bad habits. By virtue of constant repetition of your particular bad voice habits, you have come to accept the sound you make. You may even dislike it, but by and large you're comfortable with it.

It's . . . *you!*

But let's pause for a minute here, and go back to the basics, to see if I can prove you wrong.

You were born with the ability to speak. Producing sound is one of several functions of the larynx, and you probably made your first sound by entering the world with a cry.

Speech came later, for as you developed, you learned to form words and pronounce them. Your parents and teachers and peers taught you how to express yourself in sentences and then to complete your thoughts in whole paragraphs. You advanced, learned a skill or became versed in a discipline. Now, with knowledge and experience, the gift of communication is yours.

Except for one important element: You haven't yet learned, or been taught, *how* to use your *own* voice!

The voice you use is one you chose to imitate, either as a child or as an adult. It is perhaps that of your mother, your father, a role model from an impressionable period of your life. Because you lacked voice instruction, you adopted as a matter of course the inflections, rhythms, sounds of someone else. You might even have "chosen" one type of voice in an attempt to dissociate yourself from another that you consciously disliked.

Maybe your mother spoke in a shrill, abrasive voice. Reacting negatively to it, you adopted a soft whisper as a style of communication. Or did your father have a weak, passive tone? If so, you may have countered with a deep barklike sound. In either case, you're as far off the mark in producing your successful voice as the person who elected to mimic the shrill voice or the weak voice, or almost any voice, for that matter.

In all probability, the voice you habitually use is not your natural voice at all.

As I said above, you were born with the *ability* to speak, much as you were born with the *ability* to ride a bicycle, drive a car, ski down a slope, climb up a mountain, try a case in a court of law, perform surgery on a patient . . . well, the list is endless. We are all, quite obviously, born with countless abilities.

Yet you wouldn't attempt to maneuver an automobile through city traffic without first learning how to drive. It's unlikely that you would take on Mount Everest without first learning the skills of mountain climbing. Certainly, you wouldn't remove an appendix without learning surgical procedures. And so it is with almost everything we do in life. Whether self-taught with the help of instructive manuals, or educated directly by others possessed of the desired knowledge, we each realize our inherent abilities by *learning* them.

Don't you think the time has come to learn to use your natural voice to its best advantage?

A DESIRE FOR SELF-IMPROVEMENT IS ALL YOU NEED

If you are like most people, my experience shows that you depend on your voice for up to eighty percent of all communication. A good voice can serve you well. Not only does it transmit information, perceptions, emotions, and responses, it describes to the world who you are. As we discussed earlier, the sound of your voice can cause you to be reacted to in a negative manner or received in a positive light. Yet you continue, day after day, month after month, year after year, with a voice that probably sells you short.

This is because you have never learned about, or been trained in, the parameters of voice: pitch, tone focus, volume, quality, rate. You have never learned proper breath support. These are the six basic attributes of importance in the speaking voice. They are the elements which, once acquired, can produce your "right" voice.

But perhaps you are still having difficulty applying the notion of "wrong" or "right" to your own sound.

If this statement fits you, just say "umm-hmmm" out loud, lips closed, spontaneously and sincerely, as though you are agreeing with me. In fact, continue to say "umm-hmmm" whenever you read something that seems to apply to you. Or even if you come upon a thought that intrigues you.

And ponder, for a moment, the extent to which you accept right and wrong in every other aspect of your life.

There's a right way to eat which affords the maximum nutritional benefits of diet. There's a right way to exercise which produces the best results from aerobic activities. In yoga, there's a right way to breathe which renders the postures most effective. In each case, the correct practices yield psychic and physical success.

Is it not, then, natural to accept the validity of a "right" or "wrong" voice? (Remember to agree with a spontaneous and sincere "umm-hmmm" whenever you are so inspired.)

Keep in mind that the rewards derived from correct voice use can and should extend to many facets of your life experience.

BECOMING THE BEST PERSON YOU CAN POSSIBLY BE

"Nothing succeeds like success." So said Alexandre Dumas the Elder. Though he wrote the line in 1854, more than a century ago, the appeal of these four words is undoubtedly greater today than ever before. No longer do class distinctions or family lineage bar anyone from reaching the top. Success can be had by all. It is yearned for by all. But just what is "success"?

Universal in its appeal, the word "success" nonetheless conjures up a different image for everyone who contemplates it. For some it connotes fame; for others, riches. But for those given to more profundity, success relates to achieving the pinnacle of a field or expertise: A singer whose range and vocal quality is unparalleled; a leader who reaches and persuades and helps the masses; a scientist whose work results in a discovery that will have a lasting effect on society; a parent whose time and attention produce a child who will contribute positively to the world community. Success can mean all this and more.

In simpler terms, success means becoming the best person you can possibly be. And in this pursuit, Americans spare little in the way of time, energy, and thought.

It is commonly accepted that presentation of self is a key factor to success. In an increasingly competitive world, the image one projects can make the difference between acceptance or rejection.

Wardrobe says a lot, of course. Three-piece suits bespeak a professional posture. Ivy League loafers and button-downs suggest a wholesome sophistication. Designer fashions embody chic and elegance. Many in the arts and related enterprises pride themselves on a wrinkled casualness that defies the standards and morés of the Establishment. The variations are countless, but in each there is a message that declares: "This is who I am capable of being; this is what I am; this *is* me."

Meanwhile, hair has been cut and blown into place. Nails are manicured. Bodies are built up at the gym, streamlined on the track, slimmed via the current diet fad. Skin tones enhanced with facials. Among those driven to extremes, wrinkles are smoothed at the plastic surgeon's office. Ah, at last the picture is complete. Armed with a body of knowledge, a talent honed to its peak, and a "look" that sums it all up, one is ready to present oneself for judgment. "Here I am, world."

In this quest for self-improvement, in this era of self-development, however, the voice is the one detail that is usually overlooked.

And yet, the voice is your primary tool of communication.

As you have already seen, a "wrong" voice can misrepresent you. It can physically hurt you. In either case, a "wrong" voice can counteract the care and attention you have given the rest of your body.

Your "right" voice can help you become the best person you can possibly be. It is an important element of success, then, regardless of the spiritual, professional, or financial success that is already yours.

Film star Henry Fonda sought my help in attaining and sustaining the use of his right voice. So did Academy Award-winning actress Anne Bancroft. And comedienne Lucille Ball. And Metropolitan Opera basso Jerome Hines, whose problems with his speaking voice threatened his singing voice. Famed entrepreneur and art collector Norton Simon had been experiencing difficulty with his voice for thirty-five years before he came to me for voice retraining. As for the results of his therapy, he exclaimed: "It's really miraculous."

In truth, the dynamics of correct voice technique are not miraculous. They only seem that way because so few in our society know how to properly use—as well as protect—the natural gift of voice.

As you'll soon see, the fundamental elements of voice production apply to everyone. They're easy to learn. The desired result is always the same, and that is to improve the quality of the voice—to make it listenable, attractive, healthy, and effective—to give it the magical ring of success.

GREAT VOICES

The fact is, most spellbinding voices were not born of "good luck," or mystical intuition. More often than not, they are the product of a desire to learn, and the discipline to perpetuate, correct voice technique.

It's a simple process of *un*learning bad voice habits and adopting good voice habits. That's what Anne Bancroft did.

This dynamic actress was experiencing pain in her throat at a time when she was preparing her return to the stage. The pain interfered with her ability to perform. She clearly needed help if she hoped to last beyond her opening night on Broadway.

Miss Bancroft expressed some skepticism when I analyzed the source of her difficulties: She was forcing her voice to the lower throat, and breathing from the upper chest. She needed to raise her pitch, achieve facial (oral-nasal) resonance in the mask area, and learn to provide breath support from the diaphragm.

She hastened to remind me that *Golda* was opening in New York in only three months, hardly enough time, she worried, to get her voice in shape.

What she didn't anticipate was the ease and speed with which she would recover a vibrant, full voice that would carry effortlessly to the last row of the theater. (Her voice retraining also brought about a complete resolution of a small contact ulcer on her larynx, caused by misuse of her voice, that had been previously diagnosed by a Beverly Hills ear-nose-throat specialist.)

By the time she completed her voice therapy, Miss Bancroft was producing a healthy, natural sound, as well as an aesthetic quality of voice that could have been hers all along.

And now I rank hers among the great voices, the voices that, like Franklin Delano Roosevelt's, have the magic. They belong to such people as Gregory Peck, Laurence Olivier, Cary Grant. And Richard Burton, Johnny Carson, and Burt Reynolds. The late Rosalind Russell and the late Fernando Lamas.

These voices mesmerize, captivate, seduce their listeners. They command attention. They are spellbinding. But you know this, of course. What you don't know is why.

All of these voices—as different as they are, for each represents a unique personality and defines an individual character—are correctly projected from "the mask."

The mask includes the bridge and sides of the nose down to and around the lips. It is so called because in ancient Greek times stage actors, playing both male and female roles, spoke through masks that covered this part of their faces and amplified their voices.

By producing sound through the mask (as opposed to the lower throat or the nose alone), the voice opens up, becomes flexible, and is filled with expression and warmth. It has carrying power and range. Speaking through the mask gives the voice oral-nasal resonance which creates tone focus, which, in turn, gives the sound aesthetic appeal. It is correct tone focus that gives properly used voices a hypnotic effect.

Tune in to the "Tonight Show" on television and listen to the way Johnny Carson uses his voice. His manner of speech has color and versatility. He understands

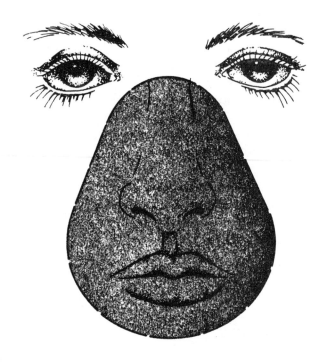

The Mask

the voice as an instrument, keeping it forward, in the mask. You'll note, too, that this healthy means of producing the voice in no way detracts from his naturally deep baritone. Indeed, it makes it fuller, richer, livelier.

All great voices are produced in this manner. They engage you and convince you. They lure you into their magical spell. They certainly contribute to success. Jack Benny had a great voice. So does Bob Hope. Power is another by-product of good voice production. Prime Minister Margaret Thatcher of Great Britain has a superbly used voice, projected through the mask with lovely resonance and clarity.

PREMIUM VOICES

By now, however, it may have occurred to you that some success stories defy my rules. You're right, of course. There do exist unattractive voices, misused voices, that generate money and visibility.

These are the voices that I call premium voices, or money voices.

The most notable American example of a money voice is that of Howard Cosell. Cosell speaks right through his nose. Sports fans from coast to coast may groan when they hear him announcing a game. But it is this nasal tone that makes him—as well as his television network—immediately recognizable. He uses his voice as a weapon.

So does Barbara Walters. She has managed to combine the worst of everything in her voice: nasal tones, hoarseness, even a peculiar speech pattern.

Yet Cosell and Walters turn a liability into an asset because the sound of their voices is so noticeably different from others'. This sound distinction instantly calls attention to them, making them identifiable.

Julia Child has such a voice. As does actress Sandy Duncan. And film critic Gene Shalit. These personalities have all managed to project voice images that are—however unattractive and displeasing to the ears—distinctive and lucrative.

Henry Kissinger's voice is manifestly his. He speaks with guttural tones from the lower throat. Such a speech pattern is disastrous, actually. It is not only difficult to listen to but can result in voice pathology.

This low pitch—called a basal or near-basal pitch

level—is defined as the lowest note on which the speaker can sustain utterance. It is used commonly as a bedroom (or sexy!) voice, as a telephone voice, as a confidential voice, and most notably as an authoritarian voice.

Kissinger's deep tone suggests authority (a suggestion that is really no more than a vocal stereotype perpetuated by our culture and the mass media, as I'll demonstrate later). But while it has many negative aspects, including a lack of carrying power, a lack of intelligibility, and a lack of flexibility, it nonetheless helps promote an authoritarian or intellectual image. And that is precisely how such a sound has managed to serve our former secretary of state.

And so, sometimes these voices that I refer to as "wrong" do further the causes of their users.

The wonderful actor Eddie Anderson, best known as Rochester on "The Jack Benny Show," earned fame and money with his raspy sound. But what no one ever mentioned was his paralyzed vocal cord, the result of too much voice strain during the years he spent hawking newspapers in San Francisco.

If yours is a premium voice, then—if it's "wrong" but has helped you get where you are today, and that happens to be some place where you want to be—use it to your best advantage. But use it cautiously and with fair warning.

I, for one, started with a voice full of negative traits. I was a Brooklyn/Bronx kid, with the accent and nasal tones to prove it. This voice did not happen to serve me well. A college speech professor insisted that I use the deepest voice possible, so I did. . . .

I went from Howard Cosell to Henry Kissinger in no time at all. This new voice brought positive comments from my professor and some girlfriends—and caused lots of problems. Forcing my voice from the lower throat irritated my larynx and finally caused voice loss. Mine was not a good voice. Nor was it a money voice. And yet, I had always been fascinated by voices, aware that some had a hypnotic effect on me.

The Lone Ranger's, for example. As a child, I listened for his voice on the radio. It had a commanding tone, pure and clear and arresting.

But it was the voice of Martin Block that made the greatest impression on me. An entire generation of radio fans will remember his as the host of "The Make-Believe Ballroom." His voice was rich and lively and totally captivating. I wanted to sound like him, but I didn't know how.

And so I eventually began a personal odyssey. What were, in fact, the fundamentals of voice success and vocal health? How were they achieved? In the years to come, I finally discovered practical solutions to my questions.

I now invite you to share in what I have learned in the past thirty-three years, and to benefit not only from my experience but from that of my former patients, patients who have joined company with the great voices, patients such as Diahann Carroll, Richard Crenna, Richard Basehart, Kirk Douglas. Also, Anne Bancroft, Norton Simon, Jerome Hines. And many more.

THE VOICE

In every voice there may be two pitch levels: an optimal or natural pitch level; and a habitual or routine pitch level which the speaker normally uses. If the speaker's "natural" (or correct) pitch is different from the pitch level routinely used, the voice is being misused. Misused pitch may be too high or too low. Americans tend to use too low a pitch.

To facilitate your understanding, imagine the throat

as a megaphone that projects the voice. Divide the throat into three areas: the lower throat, the middle throat, and the upper throat. The upper throat centers around the nose; the middle throat centers around the mouth area; the lower throat centers around the voice box or larynx. Resonance or tone focus should be produced from all three areas. Too much emphasis on any one area can create a misused voice.

For example, too much nasal resonance produces a nasal sound. Too much lower-throat resonance produces a forced, guttural sound.

Good voices have balanced upper- and middle-throat resonance—oral-nasal resonance, which I call the two-thirds solution—with natural lower-throat resonance. The area around the mouth and nose, as you will recall, is called the mask area. Tone focus in the mask makes voices sound rich, full, vibrant, and flexible.

Voice quality is affected by pitch and tone focus. Good quality may be described as clear and resonant. Misused quality can be termed nasal, thin, hoarse foggy, harsh, whiny, breathy, sharp, or squeaky, to mention a few types.

Breath support for speech should be centered at the level of the diaphragm, which is located in the midsection of the body. Upper-chest breathing, in which the upper chest or shoulders heave up and down as one breathes, is incorrect and detrimental because of the tension it creates around the throat area. Such breathing is exhausting, both physically and mentally.

Correct volume is measured by its moderate level. Volume should be produced comfortably, without strain, and should be appropriate for each situation; inappropriate volume is too soft or too loud.

Rate of speech should be easy, natural, and flexible in response to the demands of the circumstance. Fast

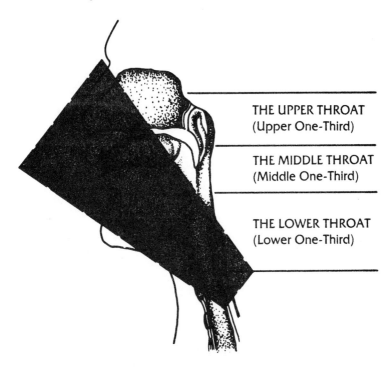

THE UPPER THROAT
(Upper One-Third)

THE MIDDLE THROAT
(Middle One-Third)

THE LOWER THROAT
(Lower One-Third)

The Two-Thirds Solution: All excellent voices are projected from the upper two-thirds.

delivery can set the listeners' nerves on edge. A slow, monotonous rate can bore listeners.

Keep in mind that the voice is an instrument that permits *animals* to make sounds. But in the human animal it is all the more precious, as it allows for speech, that is, *controlled* sounds that communicate ideas and emotions.

The *well-produced* voice commands, persuades, instructs, conveys—successfully. Because it is produced as nature intended, such a voice seldom tires and should basically never fail. It flows easily, mellifluously, enunciating thoughts in a manner that elicits attention and respect. It draws positive notice to the personality of the speaker and to the content of his speech.

If you believe, as I do, that you can and should incorporate these simple elements of proper voice production into your life, say "umm-hmmm" with your lips closed, as though you are spontaneously and sincerely agreeing with me.

If you think that mine is a voice in the wilderness speaking out on an ignored subject, say "umm-hmmm" once more.

If you wish to improve the sound you make every time you speak, say "umm-hmmm" yet again.

FINDING YOUR RIGHT VOICE

The first step in improving your voice is finding it. By this I mean locating its optimal, or natural, pitch. This is of primary importance because incorrect pitch and tone focus, used over time, are responsible for causing and perpetuating most voice misuse. Various approaches have been used to determine optimal pitch, but most have built-in flaws.

For many years, a piano was commonly used to locate vocal range. This was at best a tedious procedure and at worst impractical. Who, if anyone, is capable of carrying around a piano during the voice retraining period to sustain (or remind one of) the proper tones? In addition, it requires, if not a trained musical ear, a very good ear.

Another traditional approach, more effective than the use of a piano but still less than ideal, is the chewing method. Here, the patient is advised to chew naturally and at the same time to produce sound. This sound is assumed to be at the proper pitch level.

In some cases, this presumption is borne out. But it doesn't take long to discover that one *can* chew and make sound at an incorrect pitch as easily as at the correct pitch level. This method thus requires careful supervision of the patient, which is the element it was devised to do away with.

In addition, many people find it objectionable. They complain, quite understandably, about the abnormality of these obvious movements. And the necessity for constantly thinking of chewing becomes burdensome and distracting.

It therefore became clear that a new method was needed, one that would assure accuracy of pitch level, while at the same time affording simplicity and practicality. The device which evolved is so simple that you can carry it out yourself and instantaneously discover both your optimal, or natural, pitch level, as well as your correct tone focus. This is important since these two basic elements of correct voice technique are interdependent.

You have already, in fact, achieved this significant step of finding your right voice. If, that is, you have said "umm-hmmm" in a spontaneous and sincere manner, lips closed, whenever the material applied to you.

Try it again now. Say "umm-hmmm," using rising inflection with the lips closed. It is vital that this "umm-hmmm" be *spontaneous* and *sincere*.

The sound you are producing should be your right voice—this is your natural pitch, enhanced by tone focus.

If you are doing exactly what I asked of you, you will feel a slight tingling or vibration around the nose and lips. This indicates correct tone focus, with oral-nasal resonance.

If your pitch is too low, which occurs in most cases of voice misuse, you will feel too much vibration in the lower throat, and very little if any at all in the mask area.

Repeat the exercise, say "umm-hmmm," to deter-mine if you are doing it properly. Make a correction, if necessary, until you feel the tingling sensation about the lips and nose.

The beauty of this simple method is that it is one you can use all the time. You have countless occasions to say "umm-hmmm," when you are genuinely agreeing with someone, or when you merely want to test the pitch level you are using. This can be done in the home, in the office, while reading the newspaper, when talking on the telephone, when ordering lunch.

This is the voice you will learn to use all the time. Specific exercises will be given for sustaining this voice level and focus, and also for learning breath support. We'll look, too, at means of achieving good volume and appropriate rate of speech.

And then we'll discuss voice psychotherapy! Yes, voice images are often the most difficult "habits" of all to change.

But maybe you are not convinced of having found your (natural and physiological) "right" voice. Let's find out for certain if you have.

TWO TESTS TO GET YOU ON YOUR WAY

The "instant voice press" will almost always reveal your natural physiological voice. Standing, place your index finger just under your sternum (where your ribs come together). Now press gently with a staccato move-ment and make sound with the lips closed.

The sound you are producing is essentially the one you were born to make—the voice you were born to use.

Now say "umm-hmmm" in that same voice.

Maybe you're still having trouble.

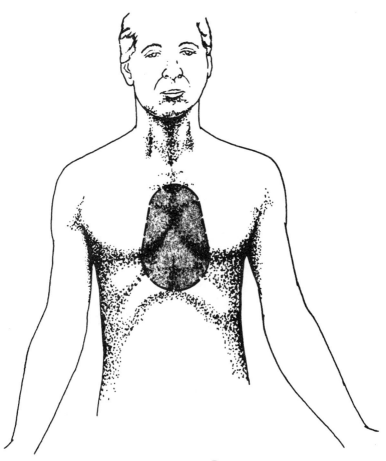

Instant Voice Press

If this is so, you've built up a physical or mental resistance to changing your voice. You may be posturing or holding yourself stiffly. So let's break that "body armor"!

Still standing, raise your hands above your head, as high as they will reach. Now say "right!" And say it again, only this time louder. "Right!" Say "hello!" in that same voice. Now say "umm-hmmm." This should be your natural voice, your right voice.

We'll get on with the business of learning to use it in a moment. But if you are already worried about employing this, your correct voice, in public or on the job, I should explain you need not be self-conscious.

In all likelihood, no one will be *consciously* aware that your voice is different, or even that it is better. That is because most of us react to deficient or unpleasant voices, in other words sounds that interfere with easy communication. Such voices call attention to themselves, negative attention that leaves the listener with a potentially adverse impression of the speaker.

Clear, dynamic, well-used voices, as we noted earlier, generate positive responses—*not* to the sound of the speaker, but to personal characteristics as well as to the content of the discussion. The properly produced voice, then, permits individuals to be perceived for their substance—physical, intellectual, and emotional.

That is the reason voice images play such a significant part in our lives. We are all greatly influenced by sound. Lovely sounds have a positive effect on our psyches. Unpleasant sounds have a negative effect. The voice, in its primitive sense, is no more than a sound.

Your natural, physiologic sound—your right voice—will bring about scant, if any, notice to itself. It will, instead, invite greater interest in who you are and what you have to say. And so, you see, there's no cause for self-consciousness as you learn to use your correct voice. Indeed, there's every reason to master voice usage.

2

The Voice You Love Could Be Your Own

YOU CAN BE BETTER THAN YOU ARE

The simple program that follows has produced excellent results in countless patients who, for various reasons, have wished to improve the functional or aesthetic use of their voices. The mechanics are easy to learn and implement. But your ultimate success will depend to a large degree on your frame of mind. You must want to be better than you are.

Almost everyone, actually, wishes to improve himself in some way. I do. You probably do, too. And well you should. We live in a society rich with opportunities for those with the drive to compete for them. But achievement of any sort—professional, physical, personal, or spiritual—generally demands that we push our talents and strengths to new limits. And so this process of advancement generally requires some form of self-improvement.

Where to turn for advice and guidance? Well, just about anywhere. Magazine and newspaper columns abound with articles. And the most prominent shelves in your local bookstores consistently feature the latest treatises on improving your negotiating skills, your business savvy, your beauty potential, your familial relationships, your sleep patterns. The list could go on and on.

There's something for everyone. But there are also inherent dangers and disappointments in getting caught up in the self-improvement frenzy that has of late gripped America.

Some people get swept away by their own enthusiasm to become super-beings. They purchase every personal advancement and make-yourself-over manual that hits the market. And then—having skimmed the highlights of each but having incorporated the finer points of none—become immobilized by their overambitiousness. They are left, embarrassingly, with impressive home libraries but no new skills.

Others err in another direction that is equally defeat-- ing. They select those self-help guides that hold the least promise for them. Instead of focusing on advice and techniques designed to enhance *their* particular talents and predispositions, they set out to make themselves over, to become someone they're not. And in the end, they too usually meet with frustration.

In either case, follow-through is inhibited by misguided expectations. And so these overachievers eventually give up and decide to join the "I've got to learn to love myself as I am" ranks.

While there is healthy logic in accepting your own limitations, this is an argument that all too often implies surrender. It is generally presented in a passive tone that bespeaks underachievement, which then neutralizes any hope for growth. And this leads us back to where we started, wishing for self-improvement; seeing, sensing, longing to partake of the endless opportunities that exist in our society, but not knowing how to effectively compete for them. And in time the cycle frequently begins all over again with misguided expectations, lack of proper direction, and ultimately, frustration.

In fact, there's no reason to be static, to be stuck in

repetitive routines, without growth. And there *is* every reason to discover that personal advancement simply requires an equal mix of self-knowledge and self-discipline.

It's important to work with the "raw" materials of the mind and body, much as you would with a piece of stone that will become a sculpture. You don't just begin chipping away in the blind hope that a majestic work of art will emerge. Instead, you begin with an analysis of the building block to reveal inherent qualities that can be exploited, as well as flaws that must be minimized or else turned to artistic advantage. A design is conceived and then a plan detailed. And of course discipline now enters as a factor, for without it no creative accomplishment can be realized.

To achieve results when wishing to further yourself, the same process should be followed. The *givens* must be established: special abilities; personal interests; liabilities; the raw materials upon which to build. A goal— a *realistic* goal—must be defined and then carried to completion.

Since we all define ourselves to an enormous extent through voice and language, and since we are all given the basic equipment to produce a commanding voice, it is not only realistic but desirable to learn to use this instrument of expression to our best advantage. As I will remind you over and over again, the voice is your primary tool of communication. If used properly, it can help you win love, success, respect, approval.

So with a bit of discipline (and that means follow-through!), you can be better than you are. You should have found your right, natural voice. Once you learn to use it all the time, you just might discover the magic you've always wished was yours.

LET'S AGREE TO AGREE

Your correct pitch and tone focus have been located by using the "umm-hmmm" method. This is the simple tool I have used for years to get my patients started on the road to voice success. Now you must begin the process of learning to speak in normal conversation using this pitch—placed in the mask and complemented with facial (oral-nasal) resonance. You need to become accustomed to the sound and feel of this natural but new voice.

To start, we'll perform a simple exercise whose only requirement is that you agree to agree with each of the sentences listed below. If you're a fiercely independent freethinker, you might find this request a bit challenging, but bear with me. I promise not to get provocative. You need only read each line silently and then respond with a spontaneous and sincere "umm-hmmm," using a rising inflection with the lips closed. If your "umm-hmmm's" are genuine, you should feel a slight tingling or vibration around the nose and lips which will verify correct pitch and tone focus.

—Winston Churchill was a noted orator and wartime leader.

—Franklin Delano Roosevelt is remembered as a president who possessed magnetism and great persuasive powers.

—I, too, would like to be skillful in the art of communication.

—My voice may be selling me short because I've never been educated to use it in an effective and healthy manner.

—For the first time, I am aware that the voice I've always used may not be the voice nature intended me to have.

—Since I would like to be the best person I can possibly be, I would be well-advised to learn the easy and straightforward technique of correct voice production.

—By disciplining myself to use my natural, right voice in everyday conversation, I can use the inherent gift of speech to my best advantage.

Did you answer "umm-hmmm" to each of the above sentences? If so, the sound you are producing should be your optimal pitch. Because it is mostly likely different from your *habitual* pitch (the pitch level you normally use), it will take some getting used to. And so we'll slowly move toward producing the same sound in conversation. Let's start with numbers.

Say "umm-hmmm-one." Now "umm-hmmm-two. "Umm-hmmm-three."

Is the pitch of the number at the same level as the "umm-hmmm"? It should be. Listen carefully to your own voice as you continue counting, preceding each number with a natural and sincere "umm-hmmm."

"Umm-hmmm-four." "Umm-hmmm-five." "Umm-hmmm-six."

Perhaps you're not certain you're speaking at the correct pitch level. So let's use our back-up method to be sure the sound you are producing is correct.

Place one hand on your chest and your other hand on your stomach and breathe in with your stomach moving out. Keep your lips closed, making a humming sound, and now press in under the sternum in a quick staccato fashion. The sound escapes through the nose, but you will feel a buzz around the mouth and nose. The resonance you feel from the mask gives the well-used voice a clear and efficient sound.

Revert to this "instant voice press" during the learning stages whenever you seem unable to locate your correct pitch level.

But maybe you find this an act lacking dignity or attractiveness? You feel it might call the *wrong* kind of attention to you? (A former patient did relate a story of having performed the "instant voice press" while in an elevator, whereupon a fellow rider felt compelled to administer cardiopulmonary resuscitation to him. And Joan Rivers—a comedian whose humor may be raucous but whose bearing is elegant and refined—*did* look appalled when I carried out the "instant voice press" on her without first explaining my intentions.) I, personally, am neither inhibited nor self-conscious about such things, but if you are, keep in mind that this is an easy exercise that requires no more than an instant. It can be executed in the privacy of your office, your car, your home—or even your bathroom, if you're one who prefers complete seclusion.

In fact, I advise most of my patients to begin each day with this routine: a few "umm-hmmm's"; some counting as described above; and an "instant voice press."

Indeed, I suggest everyone start off the morning in this way because the majority of people I encounter say they usually awake with a husky voice.

I call this a "morning voice," for it results from a good night's sleep, in which state the body is totally relaxed. This absolute relaxation allows the voice to fall to the lower throat which, as you have already learned, produces a sound that is inefficient as well as unhealthy. (The "relaxing," or depressive, effects of alcohol consumption commonly produce the same tendency, by the way. So does extreme fatigue or depression.) In any event, it *is* reasonable, isn't it, to arouse and activate one's voice each day, much as one automatically refreshes the rest of one's body upon getting out of bed.

Since most of us head straight for the bathroom upon arising, that's a good place to start. Actually, it's an ideal place, for it is there that we prepare to present ourselves to the world. We shower; shave or apply make-up; arrange our hair. We examine ourselves in the mirror to assure that we'll measure up to scrutiny. It makes perfect sense to simultaneously prepare the voice for the day ahead while performing our ablutions.

Your voice, so important in describing to the world who you are, deserves at least half as much attention as the rest of you, don't you agree?

WHAT YOU STAND TO GAIN

It is difficult, at times, to assimilate new ideas and then incorporate them into an established life-routine. To help get you motivated, let me share with you a line often used by a man who happens to be a dear friend as well as a patient: "The voice is a second face."

Gershon Lesser has the right to assume a tone of authority in stating this truism. He knows all too well that the voice one presents to the world is as important, and sometimes more important, than the face one presents to the world.

A physician who specializes an internal medicine, a licensed attorney, a media expert in his field who does several radio and television shows a week, Gershon is constantly communicating important, if varied, messages to the listeners who encounter him in his myriad endeavors. The instrument he depends on to convey his professional judgments? The voice, of course.

In dealing with patients and clients, yes, it *does* matter that his eyes reflect warmth and understanding. His scholarly demeanor no doubt makes an impact, too. But it is the effectiveness of his voice that will determine whether his pronouncements will be heard and acted upon. The opinions and instructions he delivers might well be crucial to someone's future well-being.

And in his radio broadcasts, Gershon relies heavily on his voice to captivate and inform. All the credentials in the world are not going to draw an audience, unless, that is, the magic of his voice causes his listeners to be receptive to his message. And Gershon Lesser has significant ideas to share.

Primary among his concerns is the issue of individual responsibility for one's own life, one's own actions, one's own health.

"Too many people," he says, "want others to assume control. Their family physician, for example, is often called upon to right the wrong they're doing to themselves. They may smoke too much. They may drink too much. And they don't exercise or eat properly. Then, when the body begins to react to neglect, they visit the doctor and say, 'Make me better.' Even if they generally take good care of their bodies and just happen to fall ill, many patients do not want to actively participate in the healing process. Most people want a magic pill."

Gershon has many stories to tell, but he relates one in particular about a man who came to him complaining about allergies and a resultant postnasal drip. He had been taking antihistamines which, he said, were not doing the job. He needed something stronger, more effective, because now his throat was hurting, too.

This man had been a patient for many years and had always used a low voice which, Gershon now noticed, was becoming raspy and forced. Yes, there did seem to be irritation of the vocal cords. No, this was most likely not caused by allergies or the lack of proper medication. After a careful examination, Gershon diagnosed vocal misuse and prescribed voice retraining. This simple process of learning to correctly produce his voice would resolve his problem, the physician was pleased to report, without drugs or other medical intervention. It would, at the same time, improve the quality of his sound.

It quickly became evident that this was not what the patient wanted to hear. The man made a hasty exit from Gershon Lesser's office, called the following day to have his medical records transferred to another doctor, and never again returned for consultation. Needless to say, the recommended voice therapist was not contacted.

The point is this: Too many in our society fail to realize that by assuming greater responsibility for their own fates, they could actually improve the quality of their lives. Voice, of course, is only one aspect of the larger domain of self-determination. But while some people may still find it difficult to believe that voice is an issue in success or health, those who take the time to tune in will observe the truth for themselves. They will begin to acknowledge the extent to which they judge and respond to others' "second face," the voice. And they will seek to discover the benefits of correct voice production for themselves.

That's what Gershon Lesser did when he had trouble with his own voice. He set out to achieve the sound that nature had intended him to have, as well as to protect his physical well-being.

And now that he is highly informed on the subject of voice abuse, Gershon has observed that up to 75 percent of the patients he sees in his medical practice suffer varying degrees of voice misuse. That's an alarming estimate, especially when one considers that with the information now available, voice health, indeed voice magic, can be had by almost anyone.

I LIKE YOU BETTER ALREADY

It might be beneficial, at this point, to repeat the exercises you've already learned, don't you agree? (Respond with a spontaneous and sincere "umm-hmmm.") They are simple enough and quickly performed, aren't they? (Again, let's hear another "umm-hmmm.") Now, please, count to five, preceding each number with an "umm-hmmm" at your proper pitch level. And finish off with an "instant voice press."

Using the same pitch you've just achieved, repeat the following words:

"Hello."
"Really."
"Beautiful."
"Right."
"Ready."
"No."
"Go."
"Do."

I love these words. They're what I call "energy words," because in most instances they naturally bring the voice forward, to the mask. Do you feel the difference?

Maybe you're not sure you're making the transition from your old, or habitual, voice, to your correct pitch level. The following exercise should help.

Standing, with legs straight, bend forward from the waist as far as you can. Let your head and arms dangle loosely.

Say "Right!"
"Right-one."
"Right-two."
"Right-three."
"Right-four."

"Right-five."
"Right-really."
"No."
"Go."
"Hello."
Now stand straight up again, this time with your arms stretched high over your head.
Say "Hello!"
"Right."
"Really."
"Umm-hmmm."
"Umm-hmmm-my-umm-hmmm-name-umm-hmmm-is" and add your own name here, of course.
Lower your arms to your sides and repeat the same:
"Hello!"
"Right."
"Really."
"Umm-hmmm."
"Umm-hmmm-my-umm-hmmm-name-umm-hmmm-is" and again add your own name here.

Believe it or not, I like you better already. If you are doing as I have requested, your voice should have taken on clarity, efficiency, and intelligibility. It should have found its natural sound. A sound that can carry you through the day without fatigue. Without hoarseness. It's a sound that can win you admirers, rather than detractors. A sound that just might get you hired, listened to, lusted after, cared for. With a little bit of practice, this voice can become your habitual sound.

Repetition of the exercises you've been carrying out will help you familiarize yourself with this correct pitch and tone focus. The balance between these elements has given good quality to your voice. As you make the transition to using it in normal conversation, remember to monitor yourself from time to time with a casual and sincere "umm-hmmm." This will allow you to readily reestablish proper pitch level and tone focus without missing a beat in the discussion. This "umm-hmmm" is discreet, helpful, easy. It may initially distract you from your train of thought. But after a brief period of using the method, you will effortlessly add an "umm-hmmm" to conversation without distraction.

But maybe you're already a bit uneasy about your new voice? It's not *you*, you're saying to yourself? It doesn't sound "normal"? Well, then, it's important to note that, whether your habitual voice has been too high or too low, it's been with you for a long time. Without even being aware of it, you have a long-standing, pre-conceived sound concept of yourself. It takes time to adjust to a new voice, even if it's a better voice, much as it takes time to adjust to any change in personal habit or style. We'll cover this area of resistance to a change in vocal functioning in a later chapter. You'll be surprised to discover how much you've been influenced by "voice images," and the extent to which these images have controlled the way you interface with the world.

For the time being, keep in mind that our purpose here is *not* to deny you a part of yourself, but to give magic to a part of yourself that has long been ignored.

ON BECOMING A BELIEVER

I strongly recommend at the beginning of the voice retraining period you begin each day by running through the exercises already learned. You'll find that they take only moments to do—fewer, in fact, than are required to shave or to blow-dry your hair. With the passage of time—and growing familiarity with your new voice—you'll probably find that you require only an "umm-hmmm," an "instant voice press," and a few energy words to get your voice going each morning. I also suggest you read aloud from the newspaper for just a few moments over breakfast. Before leaving for the office (or the carpool or school), every day, your "morning voice" should be replaced by a clear, efficient, and dynamic sound.

But these are solitary exercises that do not provide any feedback, or any support system for the individual. In the early stages of voice retraining, reinforcement is often important, especially for those who are resisting the alteration in pitch level and tone focus.

In my office, these concerns are easily handled.

For starters, of course, there is the ear of the therapist. That's me. I can analyze almost any voice in seconds and get the patient started on his way to voice success within instants afterward. I personally involve myself in every step of the patient's retraining. And I like to think I provide a good example of voice technique.

The use of tape recorders begins on the initial office visit, with a recording of the patient's habitual voice, as well as one of his or her right, natural voice, the voice that will be achieved with time and practice. The tapes are updated periodically. This is extremely helpful for both the therapist and the patient as replaying them reveals startling truths: "before" sounds that the patient is hard-pressed to believe are his or her own; "after" voices that show constantly improving quality and richness; documentation of a seemingly simplistic method that just happens to work in a positive way for most people. Though many individuals start off with a basic fear of tape recordings—small wonder, since the majority already dislike the sound of their own voices when played back—these recording devices eventually become a friendly and comfortable tool. They are employed until the patient's correct pitch level becomes so much a part of self-awareness that it can be maintained at will in any environment.

Another form of support offered in the office is group reinforcement. Here, patients from myriad walks of life representing nearly every type of voice deficiency meet and talk to each other. The old-timers help guide the newcomers. Conversely, the newcomers observe first-hand and reinforce the results of voice retraining in the old-timers. It's a reciprocal giving and taking that inspires confidence in all involved.

One of the most common fears expressed by those just beginning therapy, for example, is that the new voice sounds "phony." Another is that the new voice is too loud. In fact, these patients have to be continually reminded that the bones in their heads quite literally prevent them from perceiving their own voices—new or old—as others perceive them.

It took a while to convince June Claiborne.

A professional singer, June sought my help after reading an article I wrote that addressed the special problems of singers. She had lost her voice on a few occasions and she feared another episode. She seemed relieved when I explained that her singing voice would retain its strength and vibrancy (as well as its health!) once she learned to properly project her speaking voice. Yes, this suited her just fine—until she learned that she would have to abandon the husky, throaty tones with which she normally spoke.

Her new voice, she complained, seemed artificial and loud to her. Her soft platinum hair and milk-and-honey skin masked a force of personality that I was powerless to combat. Without the support of other patients, I might never have persuaded June that her correct voice did indeed have appropriate volume and was in fact prettier and more intelligible than her former (habitual) voice. She finally accepted these truths after hearing them from about twenty other patients in our constantly changing discussion sessions.

Her new voice is now consistently clear, distinctive, healthy. And she hasn't had any recurrence of problems with her singing voice either. Best of all, she's come to love her natural voice. What has she learned? That "the voice has a life of its own, if only it's allowed to function properly. . . ."

Margie Willens came to the same conclusion after voice therapy, but she carried the thought a step further.

Margie, also a singer, arranged a consultation after reading about my methods of voice technique in Metropolitan Opera basso Jerome Hines's book, *Great Singers on Great Singing.* She identified with the issues raised and correctly deduced that she might be misusing her speaking voice.

When first we met, Margie spoke in a controlled, tightly modulated voice devoid of color and nuance. And yet, curiously, she had an outgoing, assertive personality. Because she lacked proper pitch level and tone focus, the voice she presented to the world was antithetical to her character.

After hearing a tape of her old, habitual voice and her new, right voice, Margie expressed dismay: "I used to sound just like my mother-in-law, and I always thought she had a snob-affectation when she talked. I wonder if other people thought the same thing about me?" She would later describe her old sound as a "get-lost voice"; that is, a sound that served to keep others at bay.

With instructions in correct voice production, some work with the tape recorder, and encouragement from other patients, Margie quickly made the transition to using her *natural* voice in all conversation. When she expresses herself now, armed with correct pitch and tone focus, this pretty, strawberry blond has a dynamic voice that sparkles with the same intensity as her lively eyes.

"Using your *own, real* voice," she discovered, "forces your real personality to come out. It puts you on the line. It causes the world to take you seriously."

I love introducing Margie and June to new patients. They're proponents of voice health. And they're shining examples of voice magic!

THE BUDDY SYSTEM

The goal, of course, in providing a support system for the patient is to instill familiarity with the new voice, and at the same time generate confidence to employ this new voice outside the office. The most difficult part of the retraining process is the carry-over from the learning sessions to outside situations.

You may be wondering if it is necessary to simulate the conditions that exist for my office patients in order for you to make the same transition.

Is *direct* coaching from me, the therapist, a prerequisite for achieving results? Is the use of a tape recorder a necessity? Is a group support system mandatory?

Before responding to these questions, I would like to make an important point. Most of my patients would likely never have required direct vocal rehabilitation had these basics of voice production been made available to them earlier. As one former patient, Michael Waring, reported: "Most of us come in on our knees because our voice misuse has become debilitating."

In other words, you can profit from the successes of

the patients I've treated over the years by adopting my methods of voice management. Doing so should preclude your ever encountering the severity of their problems. No one should have to come in on his knees— with a voice that skips, breaks, whines, doesn't work, or sounds ugly—especially when one considers the ease with which one can acquire a commanding voice.

Keep in mind that it is only through years of treating severe voice pathology that I have refined and honed and simplified (as well as documented) the basic elements of voice production. Since these elements are fundamental as tools of communication, it would be a tragedy not to make them accessible to everyone. And this leads me to an answer to your initial question.

The patients I treat in my office are given the very same information that I am describing to you. Of course, some patients do have voice problems that have become too advanced, too severe, or too complicated for self-help. Some may be so far along in their disorders that they require surgery before beginning voice retraining. Still others are unable to or do not enjoy reading and following written directions. They prefer or need personal supervision.

But you are probably among the many who can and who wish to benefit from self-help. The secrets of commanding voice usage are neither complicated nor difficult; they have been mysterious only because they have not previously been made available to the general society. If you follow the exercises as described and use your new, right voice until it becomes a natural, easy function of self-expression, you can achieve voice magic on your own.

The use of a tape recorder might make the process move more quickly for you. You can compare and contrast your old and new sounds. You can practice and grow accustomed to your right voice by reading aloud into a recording device. You can measure your progress by replaying your tape. Any initial discomfort you feel about hearing your own voice as it really is should quickly fade as your sound becomes richer, clearer, more dynamic.

I also suggest that you establish some sort of "buddy system," which can have the same reinforcing effect as my office group sessions.

Ask your spouse or your companion to join you in the retraining process. Or a friend, or some co-workers. Or even your children. Having a partner (or partners) might prove reassuring, as well as fun. You can monitor each other's progress as well as any regression that occurs.

If, for example, you have been given to frequent throat clearing, your partner can red-light any tendency on your part to slip back into old habits. You, on the other hand, can signal a partner who slides back up to a former whine or back down to a husky croak. This human interaction might make the transition proceed more smoothly for you both.

BREATHING: FOR THE LIFE OF YOUR VOICE

Before the transition from the old or habitual voice to the new and natural voice can be successfully completed, however, you will have to learn to breathe. You already breathe on a regular basis, you say? Your very life depends on it? I don't doubt you for a moment. But the life of your voice requires that you breathe *properly.*

Would you like to perform a little test to see if you are giving your voice correct breath support?

Since I'm sure you think this is a good idea, won't you please start with a sincere "umm-hmmm." And now, if you will, count to five, preceding each number with yet another "umm-hmmm." (This constant repetition of the exercises *is* part of your retraining, as it reinforces the proper pitch level and tone focus over and over again, causing these vital elements to become ever more natural to you.)

Using this same pitch level, read aloud the following, in only one breath: "Umm-hmmm. Hello, right, really, my name is. . . . No. Go. Do."

Were you aware of your breathing? Did your shoulders move up and down during your recitation? Did your chest puff out and then deflate as you spoke? If so, you are breathing from the upper chest when you speak. It may surprise you to learn that this is a definite no-no!

Upper-chest breathing squeezes the throat area, and thus squeezes out the voice. It interferes with volume, and causes strain to the vocal apparatus.

What we want to achieve, instead, is midsection breath support. This allows for properly controlled air usage. It also takes the muscular tension away from the throat area, placing it on the abdominal muscles, which are more able to bear pressure and tension without interfering with vocalization. Correct breath support also allows for controlled volume without effort or strain.

In midsection breathing, movement should come primarily from the waist area or midsection. Your shoulders should not rise and fall, and the chest should remain still. As you breathe in, your stomach should move out slightly. As you proceed to talk, your stomach should move in smoothly and gradually. This should not be a dramatic or even outwardly noticeable gesture. Rather, it should be gentle, subtle, discreet. Breathing correctly from the midsection is invisible to everyone but yourself.

Americans are strangely obsessed with sucking in

their stomachs, this in an attempt to present a firm, flat midriff. As a consequence, I sometimes have difficulty convincing patients to abandon upper-chest breathing. Many fear that their midriffs will protrude if they breathe correctly.

This was true of one young actress who came to me for help with her voice. She had quickly mastered the elements of voice production but refused to breathe as I instructed. "I can't help it," she exclaimed of her refusal to make the adjustment. "I'm afraid no one will give me a part if my stomach is sticking out."

Her stomach wouldn't "stick out" if she breathed properly, I explained over and over again. Good posture was the key to body alignment, in any event, I told her. She wouldn't listen. On her next visit, the young actress encountered a well-known movie actress in my office, also a patient, and together we three continued the discussion of breath support.

"Is my stomach sticking out?" asked the movie star.

"No," observed the young woman, who was clearly in awe of the celebrity.

"Well, then," continued the star, "let me inform you that *I* am breathing correctly nonetheless. Furthermore, I *like* breathing correctly because it makes me feel better and sound better. I strongly suggest you do the same."

After all my coaxing, convincing, and cajoling to persuade the younger actress, how did she now respond?

"Okay," she agreed instantly. "Then I will."

And she did, without further complaint or protest.

Since most people breathe from the upper chest, this proper breathing initially seems a difficult task to learn. In fact, it's simple. Like all the other elements of correct voice production, it merely requires a few exercises and some self-awareness. After a while, it will be routine to provide midsection breath support when you speak. The following will teach you how.

Lie on your back on the floor, with one hand on your chest and the other on your stomach. Breathe in *gently* through the nose. Exaggerated deep breathing is neither necessary nor desired. Your midsection or stomach moves outward as you breathe in, with the chest remaining still during inhalation. Now exhale through your mouth. As you do so, you will feel the midsection smoothly and slowly deflate.

Still lying on the floor, breathe in now through the mouth. Feel the midsection expand slightly. And exhale through the mouth. Breathing should be soft and easy, not labored or forced.

Repeat this exercise several times while still in the supine position, and then repeat the same sequence in the standing position. Keep one hand on the chest and the other on your stomach. Start by inhaling through the nose and exhaling through the mouth. Continue by inhaling *and* exhaling through the mouth. Be aware of your midsection expanding and deflating gently and smoothly.

Once you are comfortable with midsection breathing in the standing position, proceed to a sitting position and repeat the sequence again. Remember to breathe gently. Deep breathing will tense the entire body and dry the throat.

Finally, keeping one hand on your midsection and the other on your chest, breathe in and say: "Ummm-hmmm. Hello, right, really, my name is. . . ." Feel the stomach move inward slightly as you speak. Take another gentle breath in, with the midsection expanding slightly, and say: "Hello. Beautiful. No. Go. Do."

It would be a good idea to perform the breathing exercises on a regular basis until midsection breath support is completely natural to you. You should choose a time when you are not hurried, as rushing through these particular exercises will not afford quicker results. Indeed, performing them even at a relaxed pace might cause you to feel dizzy for a moment, the result of excessive oxygen intake. This temporary phenomenon should pass quickly.

It may take a while to routinely combine the midsection breath support with tone focus in regular conversation. All you need is a little practice. A buddy or a partner is an asset here, as you can work together unselfconsciously and monitor each other. And once again, your buddy can reassure you as to the volume with which you are speaking. You may suspect that your voice is too loud when in fact it probably is not.

As I mentioned earlier, the change in pitch which you have achieved, accompanied by tone focus, has given your voice carrying power and clarity, not loudness. And now, with midsection breath support, your voice projects with such fluidity and ease that you may initially sense it is louder than it really is.

Listening to your voice on a tape recorder and comparing it to another voice recorded at the same level on the same machine should help reassure you that you have achieved clarity and strength of voice, not excessive volume.

In time, you should find your new voice projects with moderate volume in all situations, even in noisy environments. You no longer have to shout to be heard. You need not strain to be understood. Your natural voice, buttressed with breath support, has enough carrying power to be heard in most any circumstance. It always helps to face your listener when you talk.

Cheering, such as at a ballgame, is at times appropriate, but do not make a habit of it. Screaming excessively or repeatedly, too, can damage the vocal apparatus.

If you wish to have a confidential conversation, decrease the volume at which you are speaking; *do not* let your voice fall down to the lower throat. There's a big difference, one that you will increasingly understand as your right, natural voice becomes ever more a function of your self-definition.

Keep in mind that the carry-over from learning and practice sessions to outside situations will be gradual, not sudden. Initially, you may find that you cannot easily concentrate upon using your new voice without interfering with what you have to say. Or you might discover that high-pressure circumstances cause you to revert to your old voice. You may even feel self-conscious about your new voice, fearing that others may criticize the change.

In fact, few if any people will be *consciously* aware of the improvement in your voice because most of us react, instead, to negative vocal traits such as hoarseness, whininess, skips, or breaks in the voice. Good, clear, healthy sounds, on the other hand, are readily accepted and responded to in a positive manner.

So familiarize yourself with your new sound at your own pace. Become comfortable with the correct breathing technique you have learned. And let your natural voice ease itself into your life. Practice makes perfect.

THE WINNING COMPONENT IS WITHIN YOUR GRASP

We started this chapter with a general discussion on self-improvement, and then again narrowed our focus to the area of voice usage. I hope you are beginning to grasp both the significance that correct voice production can have in your life, as well as the ease with which it may be attained. The principles are probably new to you. Indeed, you're not likely to have encountered any talk on the subject before.

You have heard about educating oneself for success. About dressing for success. About physical fitness as a key to success. Even about diction as a means of conveying success. And yet the voice is your primary tool of communication in a communications-obsessed world.

The ability to communicate effectively can change your life. It can give you an edge in a competitive society. It might even give you an edge on greatness.

Churchill's words live on, years past his death. He not only conquered a handicap but became a world leader through his use of voice and language. And Roosevelt still serves as a model to be emulated by American politicians who yearn to capture the attention and stir the passions of voters. Most contenders fall short, in part because their voices do not serve them well.

And so what, you're saying? You don't seek power, fame, or glory? Your aspirations are less lofty? Well, the principles still apply to you. I've never met a person who didn't want to be liked. Who didn't want to be listened to. Who didn't want to be appreciated for his or her individuality. And that individuality—that specialness that is you—is what we're aiming to reveal in your voice.

Therein lies the essence of my message to you: Your voice is your personal trademark. It serves as a calling card, presenting you and your ideas and your personality to a judgmental world, a world that will remember your voice image as vividly as your physical image, and perhaps more vividly.

This natural, right sound that is naturally yours is now within your grasp. Yes, the lessons learned in this chapter are the prime substance of your voice retraining.

You should have located your proper pitch level and achieved tone focus. Together, in balance, these elements have created quality of sound. You have been instructed in midsection breathing which will allow you to project your new voice with controlled volume and without physical strain.

Your new voice consciousness will enable you to achieve a rate of speech that is comfortable for both you and your listeners. Moderation is your goal; speaking too slowly or too quickly can alienate others. All words in a sentence should be enunciated, but should flow smoothly, one after another, to sustain continuity. Attempt to complete one thought before articulating a new twist. Long pauses will invite others to jump in and interrupt the point you are making. The new vitality of your sound, however, will help hold the attention of others, whatever your particular rate of speech.

This has to be one of the simplest self-improvement courses you've ever undertaken. Many proponents of voice success would aver that it is also one of the most beneficial.

All that is required of you now is repetition of your various exercises on a regular basis until the variables of good voice usage are routine to you. And, perhaps, you will have to hurdle a few psychological barriers along the way. We'll get to them in Chapter 4.

But first, let's examine some of the prevailing myths and misconceptions of voice usage, as well as some of the anxiety-producing situations that can wreak havoc on the voice as well as the psyche. I hope they will give you the impetus to grab onto the intangible power inherent in your natural voice—and then use it to your best advantage.

3

Reality Training

Not long ago, I met with a successful, powerfully built businessman who told me the following story. He had always hated the sound of his own voice, which had a strange sort of perpetual gargling quality to it. It was apparent that others, too, were repelled by his voice, for they either flinched or withdrew physically when he spoke. He had years before taken to doing business by proxy, always using an intermediary to represent him in his professional dealings.

In the meantime, over twenty years, he had consulted with countless medical specialists to correct his vocal flaws. Most told him there was nothing wrong with his throat, that this was his voice and he would have to live with it. Others put him on medication, including cortisone, antihistamines, sedatives. One doctor recommended surgery in which the laryngeal nerve would be cut. Two others suggested speech therapy, which he finally elected to pursue before trying the surgery.

Various speech therapists worked with him, teaching him articulation, tongue exercises, sound repetitions. One rehabilitationist instructed him to lean forward from the waist, make noises, and run around the room "chasing" his own voice. He had not experienced any improvement. Now, having been referred by a friend, he wanted my expert opinion.

I immediately analyzed his voice. He needed to raise his pitch and speak from the mask. This we achieved with a few "umm-hmmm's," which also quickly brought about tone focus, which, in turn, imbued his voice with a smooth, rich quality. The difference in his sound was remarkable. Next, I explained, we would work on mid-section breathing so that his voice would have proper air support, as well as controlled and easy volume. These basic elements of voice production should resolve his problem.

The patient gave me a long, intense stare. Finally, reverting to his former gargle, he spoke: "If what you're telling me is true, then I've wasted twenty years and thousands of dollars on medical treatments that weren't necessary. I've run around like a chicken without a head, chasing my voice and making strange noises, and twisting my tongue into peculiar configurations. I've pumped chemicals into my body which made me depressed, sleepy, anxious, or edgy." He stood and walked to the door. Without turning to look at me before he left, he concluded, "I'm sorry, but I can't *afford* to believe it's that simple."

My first and final consultation with this patient lasted less than thirty minutes.

I tell this story because it is the sheer simplicity of my methods of voice management that strikes a chord of shock, even disbelief, in laymen and professionals alike. Medical doctors, trained to use drugs or surgery for physical deficiencies or complaints, are usually not educated in voice health. The traditionalists in my field have for years been so immersed in abstract theories, particularly as to the cause of voice dysfunction, that the fundamentals of simply producing a right voice have too often eluded them. The general public, predisposed to imagining that great voices are divinely conceived or randomly created, thus remains uninformed on the subject. Some few, such as the patient described above, have too much time and too many dollars invested in a troubled voice to accept an easy solution. So it wouldn't surprise me if you were still resistant—not to our goal, that of achieving voice magic—but to the ease with which it can be attained.

Even Anne Bancroft expressed some skepticism when I explained the course of treatment she would follow to resolve her vocal difficulties. It sounded too simple to her.

"You should wear a tweed jacket, smoke a pipe, sport a beard, and speak with a slight German accent," she said. "You should say it will take you months to understand the voice and additional time to help me."

Yet Anne progressed quickly with the basic tools of voice usage taught to her. So did actress Cheryl Ladd. And Norton Simon.

I am not suggesting, mind you, that the problems resulting from poor voice usage are less than dramatic. The businessman above who produced a constant gargle whenever he opened his mouth to speak did indeed have a weighty and confounding problem: an inability to communicate effectively. He was embarrassed by his manner of speech. As a consequence, he had isolated himself from the world. Yet he wouldn't abandon the notion of there being a mysterious cause and a costly resolution to his vocal defect.

I would like to remind you, and here I quote Thomas Mann, that "order and simplification are the first step toward mastery of a subject—the actual enemy is the unknown."

Voice health and rehabilitation is a relatively new field, and so it is a subject that has been always clouded by the enemy, the unknown. But now, thanks to order and simplification, the basic elements of proper voice production have been identified and defined. They have been described to you, along with the exercises that can produce your right and natural voice. But this voice will become your habitual sound only if you use it regularly, conscientiously applying the tools you have acquired until, at last, successful vocal techniques are second nature to you.

This all sounds quite straightforward and it is—except for one crucial factor called attitudes. Yes, your ultimate success in finding voice magic will require, in addition to changing your sound, that you change your attitudes. Attitudes born of misinformation, or indeed of *no* information. Cultural attitudes that create and perpetuate vocal stereotypes. Attitudes centered around instruments (the telephone!) and circumstances (public speaking!) that instantly spark anxiety or fear in the speaker.

In time, we will enter into a discussion of voice psychotherapy. We'll look at the ways in which images influence the way we use our voices. For now, let's examine some of the misconceptions about the voice that have previously influenced us all, and which have compelled us to vocally present ourselves to the world as we have.

Information and knowledge are liberating, and should inspire healthy change. So if you keep an open mind, you may well meet up with your own voice idiosyncracies in the pages that follow. And you might just elect to give freedom to your psyche, as well as your voice, in the pursuit of commanding, effective communication.

WHICH VOICE TYPE ARE YOU?

Since most of us were not educated in the proper use of our natural voices, we all, along the way, adopted a sound which became "our own." This sound, in fact, is rarely an individual's "right" voice. Rather, it represents, in one fashion or another, a commitment to the cultural norms of the society and/or to the stereotypes that individual has observed as being correct for a certain station, position, or situation.

A voice type may be consciously or unconsciously acquired, but in either event is indicative of a sound concept with which the user is comfortable.

If, for example, a voice type is consciously manipulated, the individual may have adopted this voice because others have commented favorably upon it. Or perhaps it fulfills an image role and vocal identity by sounding like the type of voice a person in a certain class or position or of a certain age should have.

A voice type might be *un*consciously acquired because the individual has simply imitated the voice of a friend, or, more often, of a family member. Sometimes a cold or an illness initiates a voice type which remains after the cold or illness has passed. Personality needs are frequently revealed through the voice, as when a shy person speaks quietly, or an insecure person uses the loud voice of authority to appear secure.

However your habitual (former) voice was created, it was most likely affected by a lack of voice knowledge and by poor vocal models in all areas of society, including the family, the schools, the office. And let's not leave out the mass media, which encourage and perpetuate voice stereotypes.

The *intimate* or *confidential voice*, for instance, is generally regarded by society as a good voice. This type of voice almost inevitably results in the use of the basal or near-basal pitch, which, as we previously noted, lacks carrying power, intelligibility, and flexibility. Yet it is thought to exude low-key confidence in addition to creating the impression of intimacy. It is often used by those who wish to be preceived as sophisticated, cultured, knowledgeable, in control.

Many professional people seem to feel that this lower-throat "just-between-you-and-me" sound is a must. Doctors deem it necessary for effecting a good bedside manner. Lawyers use it to establish power. Executives find it suggests discretion in talking over business deals. Telephone operators often use this voice. And so do telephone salesmen, disc jockeys, and broadcasting personalities.

Initially, the intimate or confidential voice is used in special situations for short periods of time. Unfortunately, it frequently is progressively used in more and more situations until it becomes the habitual voice of the user. Even when the voice grows husky from the constant strain on the vocal mechanism, and listeners cannot hear or cannot understand what is being said, the speaker tightens his lower throat and forces this voice, further straining his vocal folds. Curiously, this voice type is often imitated.

The *telephone voice* has two prominent types, one of which is the confidential voice described above, transferred to the electronic medium. Here, in stressing intimacy, or a desire not to be overheard, the user often drops to the basal pitch which then, as above, carries over to other speaking situations. Because society endorses this sound, it, too, is often mimicked.

The other type of telephone voice is the loud or vociferous voice. Those who make many phone calls, particularly long-distance calls, often adopt this type of voice, which utilizes too high or too low a pitch level, too much lower-throat resonance, and excessive volume. This voice is seldom emulated and does not carry over frequently to other speaking situations.

The *sexy* or *bedroom voice,* on the other hand, not only carries over to become a habitual voice, but is very contagious. It is emulated by vast numbers of people because it is encouraged and utilized by a large percentage of performers in the mass media. This voice is a synthetic or counterfeit voice acquired and used with a conscious purpose, and that purpose is to generate sexual appeal.

The individuals who use the sexy voice all conform to an obvious stereotype. This voice, when broken into its component aspects, reflects itself in a limited volume, poor and effortful carrying power, a hoarse, husky, breathy tone, and a pitch level which borders on being a monotone. To achieve the so-called sexy voice, the speaker almost invariably drops to the basal-pitch range, places the tone focus in the lower throat, and usually incorporates a breathy quality.

The *authority voice* is a role voice, too, used to conform to society's notion of what a figure of authority should sound like. Professionals in the fields of law, medicine, engineering, and education, as well as executives and administrators in all disciplines, usurp this voice, which uses the deepest level of their potential range.

Why, you ask, do people do this to themselves? Why, indeed, do people subject others to this sound? It's all part of a mythology that has taken root in America that "authority speaks low." Authority, too, it seems, prefers to conform to the norm.

Actually, the individual who adopts this voice apparently requires it as a form of self-validation. In other words, he or she does not feel representative of a high station unless this voice type is used. This belief is without point or purpose, of course, since a professional or executive title in and of itself bespeaks authority. Yet we all run into this voice type time and again in our dealings with the various professionals in our lives, who generally make this sound a habitual voice.

That's what attorney Fred Simpson of Greenwich, Connecticut, innocently did. And it may be true that this voice type worked positively for him over the short term, reinforcing his image of what a successful young lawyer should sound like. Unfortunately, it was not, over the long run, a successful sound.

His voice grew thick from the strain placed on his vocal mechanism; then in time it failed him. He is now learning to use his natural voice—a strong, dynamic baritone that will present him to clients and law partners with vigor, clarity, and intelligibility.

Like Fred, Ginger Franklin naively adopted a voice type approved by society but which caused her difficulties when used over a long period. A San Diego realtor, Ginger incorporated both the sexy voice and the telephone voice. Because she was forcing a deep sound that was not physiologically right, she eventually developed a constant ache in her throat and chest, coupled with an overriding sense of fatigue. These symptoms have been resolved since she learned to project her voice from the mask. Best of all, she not only accepts her new, natural sound—she loves it. "This voice works *for* me," she said with a wide, pretty smile, "in my working life, in my personal life. I feel better and I sound better. That's a lot, isn't it?"

Neither Fred nor Ginger was aware of voice misuse upon initiating a voice type. Each simply discovered a sound that fulfilled an immediate need and allowed it to become a habit. Joan Rivers did the same thing when the question "Can we talk?" became her comedy trademark.

Scampering across a stage in her high heels and glittering beaded gown, she pauses and poses the question. If you are in a club populated by hundreds or among a television audience numbering in the millions, you know Joan is sharing an intimacy with you and you alone. That's because in uttering the words, "Can we talk?", her voice drops to a "confidential" pitch. Therein lies the likely source of Joan's sporadic voice loss.

As with so many in our society, this voice type, forced from the lower throat and used for special situations, became her habitual voice.

In fact, Joan can have her confidential voice. You can have your authority voice. Ginger can have her sexy voice. Nature allows for these sounds—*if* they are projected from the mask, rather than from the lower throat. The intonations you put into your natural voice can reveal sex appeal, discretion, intimacy, importance— whatever trait best defines you—better than your former, misused voice.

Joan Rivers is now aware that if she hopes to maintain her voice *and* her frenetic schedule of appearances, she must learn to use her confidential voice correctly, placing this sound in the mask. She uses the same "technology" you are using, by the way.

She, no less and no more than you, does not want her voice to sell her short. Effective, successful communication is at the heart of the matter, whatever your professional or personal calling in life.

THE HIGHS AS WELL AS THE LOWS

So far, we have spent a good deal of time talking about voices that are projected primarily from the lower one-third, or the lower throat. These voice types tend to be not only accepted, but encouraged, by society. As a result, they are often imitated with conscious manipulation, and so deserved special attention. But this is not to suggest that *high-pitched* voice types are any more natural, or "right," or desirable.

Indeed, high voices are the bane of Western society. Voice prejudices *do* exist and those people who employ a high or squeaky voice are not only often dismissed or ignored, but also frequently ridiculed. To be possessed of such a sound is at best discouraging, and at worst humiliating. Keith Butler is one who knows all too well the pitfalls of this voice type.

A tall, lean, thoughtful man, Keith had had for as long as he could remember a high-pitched, thin voice. He had forever been dissatisfied with this sound which, when he heard recordings of it, revealed itself to be squeaky and thin. Try as he did to play games with his voice, he couldn't seem to maintain a deeper sound. This was because his voice type tends to constrict the lower throat when speaking (as with the basal-pitch type voice)—but then push the sound to a high pitch. The pattern becomes so ingrained, as with most vocal habits, that the individual feels helpless to break free of it.

Though aware of the unattractive qualities in his sound, Keith felt trapped by a voice he could not control. And he became increasingly concerned that people didn't seem to pay any attention to him when he spoke. He was frequently interrupted in the middle of a sentence. On occasion, the person to whom he was talking would simply walk away, oblivious of his words, oblivious even of his presence. This was not the way Keith wished to be received by his friends and acquaintances. He correctly discerned that his voice caused him to be perceived as a weak, ineffectual man.

This patient sought my advice after hearing me address a professional group. Using the same methods described to you—a few "umm-hmmm's," the "instant voice press," energy words, midsection breath support, and group encouragement—we lowered Keith's pitch, put resonance in his sound, added volume. His gentle, unassuming personality is now complemented by a voice that engages his listeners' interest.

"Without ever mentioning the difference in my voice," said Keith, "which I guess no one ever noticed, the people at work suddenly stopped looking through me and around me, as though I weren't there. They started treating me like the 'house scholar.' "

NASALITY ISN'T NICE

Another prevalent voice type that is frowned upon by society is the *nasal voice.* Such a voice is produced from the upper one-third, or the nose area. This sound, which typically grates on the nerves of the listener, is seldom if ever consciously emulated. It is, however, frequently acquired as a product of environment. Where parents speak in nasal tones, children often do, too. And nasal voices are common in certain geographical regions where they are passed on generation to generation among most of the citizenry.

I treated a famous movie star who had acquired his early nasal sound in the Midwest, where he was raised. He was simply imitating the society around him. Later, influenced by his status as a leading man as well as by Hollywood's notion of how a male star should sound, he pushed his voice to the basal-pitch range. Though he and his directors believed this deeper sound more impressive than his nasal tones, it eventually had an adverse effect, causing prolonged hoarseness and finally voice loss. Unable now to push his voice back up to a higher range and realizing that he wouldn't be able to return to work without a voice, he sought my help.

He recovered his voice use by learning to project sound from the mask.

This film actor had always been a brilliant communicator of characters' emotions and actions. It was only later in life that he came to use his voice to his own best advantage. But he had always been fascinated by the magical effect of well-used voices. Like most people, however, he simply lacked the information he needed to achieve a sound that was at once commanding and healthy.

Others, who are not attuned to sound, are less aware of their own voices. John Nevens was one of those people.

What makes his case unusual is that it was his friends and colleagues who told this medical doctor that his voice was not serving him well. An astute professional, John was nonetheless surprised when told that others had trouble understanding what he was saying. A transplanted New Yorker, he attributed this apparent lack of intelligibility to his native accent.

In fact, his vocal deficiency resulted not from his accent at all, but from his hypernasal and high-pitched voice. Lowering his pitch, projecting his voice from the mask, and using midsection breath support imbued John's voice with a smooth, clear sound that brought immediacy, attention, and intelligibility to what he had to say. An articulate man, he now has the tools to produce an effective voice. You might be surprised to learn, though I was not, that John's new tone focus had a secondary benefit: It shed, without his even knowing it, John's New York accent. But we'll discuss accents in greater depth later.

Attorney Herbert Fields, on the other hand, had long known that his communicative skills were lacking. "Even my grammar school teachers didn't like me," he said. What he didn't know was why.

Herbert, like John, had a hypernasal sound that alienated his listeners. It was only after a girlfriend's mother complained about his voice that he sought help in improving his sound. Again, we lowered his pitch, gave oral-nasal resonance (thereby diminishing the nasal emphasis and balancing the resonance), and added correct breath support to his voice.

Herbert has a new girlfriend now, and her mother just happens to love his voice.

VOICE SCHIZOPHRENIA

You may have recognized your own voice type as an intimate or confidential voice; a sexy or bedroom voice; an authority voice; a high squeaky voice; a nasal voice. You might even adopt a telephone voice the moment a phone receiver nears your ear. Or, you may be among the many who suffer from voice schizophrenia—vocal confusion resulting in the use of a different voice for every occasion and every encounter. It's a sort of revolving door of sounds with a different pitch and quality of voice emerging in haphazard fashion. Voice schizophrenia results from the lack of a clear vocal identity.

Most people, actually, have at least one *second* or *put-on* voice, used for special people or for special occasions. This is a sound that is artificial in pitch, tone focus, quality, volume, or rate, used intermittently and briefly.

Do you, for example, use the same voice when speaking to your parents that you use when talking to colleagues? Do you have a certain voice for children and another for contemporaries? Do you have a particular voice reserved solely for your pets?

A put-on voice occurs when an individual switches voice type from one situation to another, knowingly and purposefully, for the effect it has upon the listener. Such a tendency is fine as long as the second voice (or third or fourth, as the case may be) is placed in the mask, within the right range, and is buttressed with breath support.

But one danger of using a second voice is that the speaker will lose his connection with his real, right voice and then adopt a permanent sound—such as an authority, sexy, nasal, or high voice—which then routinely presents him to the world in a less than successful manner.

The other danger of changing one's voice to fit the circumstances, as mentioned above, is the potential for voice schizophrenia. Here the individual eventually develops such a plethora of voices that neither he nor his listeners have any consistent concept of who the speaker really is. In time, the uniqueness of such a person fades into a lack of definition. It's like being a nonperson, which none of us would choose as a self-image.

Yes, we do change roles throughout the day. Yes, we are different people in different circumstances. Variations of intonations are inevitable *and* proper—as long as the voice is kept in the mask, as long as the sound is authentic.

And so, time and again, we get back to this very important point: We each, as special and unique human beings, have a sound that is physiologically right; this sound, used in harmony with our personalities, is our tool for communicating with a judgmental society that records, and remembers, and rewards appealing uniqueness.

I don't want to be a "type." I don't imagine that you do, either.

SINGERS BEWARE!

"It's a Heartache" was a hit recording in 1981. If you recall the song, you might well remember, more vividly than the lyrics or the tune, the raspy, anguished voice of vocalist Bonnie Tyler. Her sound gave urgency, as well as a sense of tragedy, to her lament. And it was very effective indeed. She hit the charts in no time at all, in large part due to her forced, basal-pitched voice. I only hope this singer doesn't use this sound as her routine voice in either her music or her speech.

"It's a Heartache" illustrates more graphically than any other example I can imagine, the pathos of a voice projected from the lower throat. It's sad rather than uplifting; rough instead of smooth; deadening, not dynamic. Yet this voice type, as we already have seen, is commonly emulated by many in our society, including singers.

Rock vocalists, actually, make up the largest group of singers to use this lower-throat sound in their music. But that helps explain why so many in the rock field have short-lived careers. Their voices simply can't withstand the constant abuse and so they cease to function. Theirs is a here-and-now sound without thought or safety for tomorrow. Janis Joplin, ironically, had such a voice.

Country and Western singers, on the other hand, rarely lose their voices from years of vocalizing. That's because of their overemphasis on nasal resonance, which, though unpleasant to some ears, does not damage the voice mechanism. Their careers tend to endure for the long run.

But there is a potential fallacy in each of these generalizations which I hope you have been perspicacious enough to anticipate: Yes, each broad statement presupposes that the singing voice used is the same as the speaking voice.

In other words, a well-used speaking voice might protect to some degree an abused singing voice. But more significantly, and this is a more common phenomenon, a misused speaking voice will adversely affect a good singing voice.

That's what almost happened to Stevie Nicks of the rock band Fleetwood Mac, who is a natural when it comes to singing. She has a sound and style that quickly catapulted her to stardom. But her speaking voice was in the lower throat, forced and misused. Stevie recognized that the negative symptoms of her speaking voice might harm her singing voice, a consequence she couldn't risk. Her ear-nose-throat doctor referred her to me.

I had little time to work with her because she was preparing to go on tour. We quickly corrected her speaking voice by raising her pitch into the mask. Tone focus was achieved and breath support learned. But with the mechanics accomplished—using the same techniques described to you—I had to worry about the carry-over of her correct speaking voice to outside situations.

On the road, Stevie's voice would frequently be competing with sound distractions, such as crowds, equipment noises, the band's music. The constant travel from city to city would result in a lack of sleep. The pressure would be intense. It would be difficult to concentrate on using her new speaking voice. Our solution was simple.

We brought in a partner, or "buddy," whom we quickly trained in voice technique, to monitor and check Stevie's speaking voice. She traveled with the band and its entourage, encouraged Stevie in the use of her natural right voice. This coaching made Stevie's transition from using her former habitual voice to her correct voice proceed smoothly.

Diahann Carroll is another famous singer who experienced vocal distress even though her singing voice was beautiful as well as successful. But Diahann developed many negative voice symptoms that eventually hurt her singing voice, too. Unfortunately, it took her a good deal longer than Stevie to find the answer to her problems.

A medical doctor who treats many singers had long ago prescribed cortisone to deal with recurrent laryngitis. As far as Diahann was concerned at the time, she had found a miracle drug. Within an hour or two after taking it, her voice would sound clear. She continued with the cortisone for years and often found that she couldn't make a performance without it. But she noticed changes that concerned her. She described these changes at our initial meeting.

"I found a change in my singing range; it's become smaller. The other apparent difference is a kind of slight raspy quality all the time, which I suppose I'm so used to now that I don't even call it hoarseness anymore. I have heard recordings of myself from before, that's why I say . . . there was a definite change, not only in the singing, but in the speaking voice as well."

In addition, both she and her family physician were now becoming concerned about her prolonged use of the cortisone, which has many potentially dangerous side effects. She only used the drug when working, Diahann said, then added: "There have been times when I've worked some thirty-odd weeks out of the year. . . ."

Diahann's speaking voice, like Stevie Nicks's, was down in the lower throat, with the pitch range hugging bottom. All she needed was a voice lift. Raising the pitch put her voice in the mask. Within minutes, we had placed her voice correctly and focused it. Because, like most singers, she has a good ear for sound, she was able to hear and carry over the new voice very quickly.

Don't imagine that these problems are unique to rock or pop singers. Even an exquisitely trained singing voice can suffer if the speaking voice is being misused.

Gifted operatic star Jerome Hines sought my help years ago for voice difficulties. Despite years of vocal training and professional experience, he was encountering negative symptoms which alarmed him: "I was doing a lot of public speaking and public speaking wasn't very good for me. In fact, I found that speaking for forty-five minutes could be much worse on me than, let's say, singing concerts on two or three consecutive days. Naturally, when one particular set of muscles gets overtired from speaking, it's going to affect the singing, too."

Though his singing voice had always been in top form, this great talent had never been instructed in the proper use of his speaking voice. He was talking with a basso-profundo voice, at the very bottom of his range.

I raised his pitch only two notes, which brought about a quick accusation. "Are you making me into a girl?" he demanded in a booming bass baritone. This was a comical moment, of course, in hindsight, though at the time I was more than a bit intimidated. I explained that this very slight change would assure the good health of his voice.

Because he was highly motivated to successfully master the simple elements of voice technique, Jerome agreed to make this slight alteration in his speaking voice. In no time at all, his right voice became his habitual voice.

Even if you aren't a professional singer, your singing

voice can benefit from, and be protected by, the correct use of your speaking voice. Perhaps you are a member of a church choir, or of a community chorus. You might well discover a clearer, more colorful sound in your music after only a short period of proper voice usage. And if you are one of those people who would love to sing in the shower, but have always considered yourself tone deaf, well, there's good news for you, too.

My work has revealed that very few people are, in fact, tone deaf. Further, I've discovered that most people have very satisfactory singing voices—voices just longing to be set free. By now, it shouldn't surprise you to learn that musical expression may come quite naturally to you once you have mastered the basic elements of voice technique. Yes, finding your right voice and using it until it becomes your habitual sound will likely liberate the singing voice you never knew you had.

THE PHONE AS A FRIEND

It goes without saying that the telphone is here to stay. It also goes without saying that, by its very nature, communication via wire will never afford the advantages of face-to-face interaction where sight, smell, and touch contribute to making, as well as forming, an impression. The telephone allows only one stimulus to work for or against you: that of sound. The result is that the instrument itself becomes a kind of adversary, even if on a subconscious level. The truth is that most individuals manifest fear or loathing by playing games with their voices as soon as telephone conversation is initiated.

Such game playing is okay if you have mastery over your own voice, with placement in the mask. But it can be detrimental if you, like most people, drop your sound to the lower throat. Besides reducing the effectiveness of communication, it misrepresents the speaker and distracts or alienates the listener—who is at the same time trying to manipulate his or her own voice because of a desire to impress or persuade or convince. This is a losing tactic used by many.

However impersonal, telephonic communication is going to remain in our lives. For some, it's a sole means of carrying out business. For others, it provides a vital link to loved ones far away. And for all of us, it is a necessary connection to the countless services, stores, and people we deal with on a day-to-day basis. It's time we learned to use it to our best advantage. The telephone should serve us, not intimidate us. The crucial factor, then, is the effectiveness with which we use the gift of voice.

Your *natural* voice, the one you are learning to use, is your right voice—for the telephone, as well as for your personal encounters. It is dynamic, smooth, clear, efficient, in any and all manners of communication. It can portray you and your ideas in the most captivating way, even if your listener can't observe your warm smile, share a firm handshake, or be seduced by the scent of your favorite perfume.

No, you needn't yell to be heard, even on long-distance calls, if you are employing the elements of correct voice production. You don't have to drop to the basal range in order to sound authoritarian or sexy or intimate. Such a tendency, if projected from the lower throat, will distort or muddy your sound, thereby causing you to be misheard, misunderstood, or dismissed. You need only speak into the receiver as though it were a friend sitting across from you.

And indeed, soon after you start using your right and natural voice, you may well find new friends sitting across from you, friends so taken with your phone presence they can't resist sharing a firm handshake.

AN AUDIENCE CAN WANT TO LOVE YOU

Nothing, not even the telephone, instills as much fear and anxiety as public speaking. Whether your audience consists of 500 strangers, 50 PTA acquaintances, or 15 business associates, you are likely to dread taking the podium. The anticipation causes your palms to sweat, your heart to beat quickly. You worry about your appearance, fret over losing your composure. You try to control your nervousness by privately rehearsing your prepared speech. Finally, standing before your gathering, you open your mouth to speak.

What emerges is a forced authority voice, projected from the lower throat. This is the sound you deem appropriate—why else would anyone pay attention to your text? The problem is, your throat goes dry from pushing your voice to the lower one-third. You clear your sound, and continue. Then, horror of horrors, your voice cracks. You clear your throat again, but when you talk you constrict the lower throat, force the sound, and it emerges as a high, thin squeak. . . . By now, consumed by the negative image you are presenting, you've lost your train of thought.

This "dramatization" is an exaggeration, of course. But not too much of an exaggeration, for the bare reality is that most individuals do assume poses, put on second voices, and agitate over images whenever they are speaking before a group. Such posturing is usually self-defeating.

An audience will, in fact, want to like you if only you present yourself honestly, openly. When called upon to address any size audience, then, *be yourself!*

If you are a shy, reflective person, speak from the heart, but with your right voice. You will probably touch a few other hearts, and win them over to your cause. If you are an extroverted individual who enjoys provoking and challenging others, let your personality shine through. When you have fun, so, too, will your listeners.

If you approach such an engagement with this attitude—that you are going to present yourself as you really are—you need concern yourself with only two criteria to insure your success.

For starters, you must simply know your subject. If you are familiar with your material, you will not even need a prepared speech. Simply make a list of the most important points you wish to cover. Always begin an address by telling your listeners why your topic is important and how it might impact upon their lives.

If ever you get stuck, ask for questions from the floor. Questions will no doubt remind you of any details you forgot to mention, and will also give others an opportunity to express their concerns or their own points of view, thereby taking the attention away from you for the moment.

If the sea of faces staring at you begins to distract you from your subject, find a few friendly gazes in the audience to talk to. And address those people as if they were sitting in your own living room. No one else will know the difference, and you will be able to proceed as though in a comfortable, friendly discussion. This will allow you to feel more natural, more spontaneous.

But if you truly hope to be perceived as natural and spontaneous, it is imperative you use your right voice. Yes, I'm referring to your OWN voice, projected from the mask with oral-nasal resonance and midsection breath support.

Almost anyone can spot a *poseur*—and this applies to any speaker who is putting on airs *or* putting on voices. A forced or phony sound can prove as distracting to an audience as it is to the speaker. It can even be alienating.

And so this second criterion of successful public speaking leads us back to our primary goal: voice magic. Once again, allow me to remind you that a well-used voice is a reflection of the best you have to give. And we all want to give our best.

ACCENTS: LOVE 'EM OR LEAVE 'EM

I happen to love some accents: French accents, and soft Southern accents, in particular. They are colorful, as well as charming. In fact, I often find myself trying to convince certain patients *not* to modify or lose their regional or national intonations. One such patient was a native Frenchman who believed his accent prevented him from being accepted as a nationalized American citizen.

But this gentleman sounded like Charles Boyer, who had an exceptionally well-produced voice as well as an engaging accent. I couldn't bring myself to help the patient with his request. It took some cajoling, but I eventually persuaded him to leave his voice alone. It was a cultured, sophisticated, captivating voice.

Some accents—such as Midwestern twangs, syrupy Southern drawls, heavy foreign or ethnic phonations, New Yorkese—often inhibit an individual's social or professional mobility, however; I treat dozens of such cases each year.

The emphasis these days is on regional anonymity. Most people want to sound as if they came from nowhere. They don't want to stand out as being from a particular place or culture. They simply wish to be accepted. And it is true that accents sometimes call attention to an individual's origins rather than to what he or she is saying.

A chief executive with a major corporation consulted me in order to lose his New York accent, which some of his friends and colleagues found threatening. He spoke like a mafioso don stereotype before therapy neutralized his sound.

Another executive, this one a Chicagoan who had moved to San Francisco fifteen years earlier, told me he was still viewed as an outsider in his company because his accent set him apart. Soon after he modified his accent, he was promoted to a new position.

When treating such patients, I initially concentrate on improving the voice—locating the correct pitch and creating tone focus and achieving correct breath support. Here we use the very same methods of proper voice production already learned by you. And what often happens—as it did with John Nevens, the New Yorker with a hypernasal sound—is that the accent is so diminished that it seems to have vanished.

For those who feel their accents, either foreign or regional, are too noticeable, articulation therapy is initiated. Work is done on individual speech sounds and on intonational patterns. This, like other aspects of voice retraining, requires concentration and discipline until new habits—successful habits—are formed. But the process is easy if the individual has the motivation to go after his or her goal.

Along the way, the patient is advised to become more aware of diction, to use "-ng" endings in words, for example instead of "n," for example to say "running," instead of "runnin'." Midwesterners and New Yorkers, in particular, need to alter the sound of their vowels, to say "many" instead of "miny," to say "back" instead of "beck."

I suggest you not worry about your accent unless you believe it gets in the way of social acceptance or advancement on the job. You may even find that when your family and friends hear your new and proper speaking voice with its greater resonance, they will think you have already softened or lost your accent.

Most importantly, keep in mind that I work with sound every day, and I usually find that it is a *voice* that needs improvement, not an accent. Accents can give flavor and color to a well-used voice. Cary Grant has a beautifully used voice and an elegant English accent. I wouldn't change either for the world. Henry Kissinger has a poorly produced voice and a German accent. I would love to change his sound, but not his accent. Yes, that's right. Kissinger's German accent would suit him and his personality just perfectly if his voice were improved, raised to the mask and buttressed with midsection breath support.

If you have an accent, you can love it or leave it. The choice is yours to make. As you will soon come to understand, the deciding factor will rest in your self-image. By this I refer not only to your own sense of who you are—but also to the way you wish to be perceived by the world.

4

Destroying the Myths

SELF-IMAGE = VOICE IMAGE = SELF-IMAGE

The six parameters of healthy, dynamic, successful voice usage are physically easy to achieve, as I have hoped to demonstrate to you. They represent the mechanical side of the issue. As I've stated, almost everyone is capable of mastering these mechanics—once the elements are understood and implemented—and using them as an effective, arresting tool of communication.

On the surface, then, there's nothing to hold you back, nothing to prevent you from making the transition to captivating communication skills. But beneath the surface, there always lurks the psyche, and the psyche is capable of presenting all manners of mental barriers to personal or physical change.

These psychological barriers thus play a significant role in the success or failure of your voice retraining. They manifest themselves primarily in what I call "voice images."

A voice image is a sound or voice that an individual either likes or dislikes, either identifies with or refuses to identify with. It has nothing to do with the natural vocal abilities of the speaker, but rather is formed essentially by the culture around him: the peer group; the family; the mass media. That is why, as we discussed in the last chapter, voice stereotypes abound in our society.

Society, for the most part, endorses a sound projected from the lower throat and rejects the high-pitched and the nasal tones. But neither represents a well-placed sound. Neither serves the individual well. Yet attitudes toward these sound concepts are pervasive in our culture because so few people understand the elements that actually produce a well-used voice. As a result, the public accepts and assimilates without question these attitudes, thereby perpetuating an ill-conceived and misbegotten code.

But when the negative symptoms of any voice type become so pronounced as to blatantly interfere with communication, society rebels—curiously, not against the misinformation that has guided too many of us, but against the speaker who has been victimized by a voice image that has failed to serve him well.

What we are talking about is a circular, spiralling movement: A misinformed society inculcates voice stereotypes; the individual consciously or unconsciously adopts one of these voice types which becomes rooted in the psyche as a personal voice image; the individual outwardly projects and thus fulfills the general characteristics of his or her voice type; the voice used is ultimately unsuccessful because it lacks aesthetic appeal or clarity or efficiency; the society in time rejects the individual who uses the voice type that the society initially inculcated.

Who is the loser here? The individual who knowingly or unknowingly adopts a voice stereotype, and that includes most individuals in our society. Who, in the end, is the winner? The person who decides to transcend voice stereotypes and learns to use his or her *natural* voice in a manner that will project a *positive voice image.*

Susan Rhodes had been petite and shy all of her life. She adopted a "little" voice early on—a high, thin sound that generated scant interest in her because it kept others at bay. This lack of attention from the people around her reinforced her shyness, which, in turn perpetuated the use of her lackluster voice. Even though society accommodated Susan's negative voice image by treating her as an insignificant person, what she secretly wanted, as do we all, was to be loved, noticed, appreciated.

Here you can see, then, that Susan's voice image reflected her self-image, which nurtured her voice image. She was on a merry-go-round that might never have stopped.

Then Susan came upon voice therapy purely by accident when she attended a management seminar where I had been asked to talk about the voice as a tool for professional success. Realizing that her weak voice might eventually inhibit her career growth, Susan sought my help. In no time at all, we had lowered her pitch and added balanced tone focus, which gave resonance to her sound. We worked on breath support and increased her rate of speech, which had been boringly slow. We played back a recording of her new sound.

"How do you like your new voice?" I asked.

"It's a great voice," she answered, "but it's not me."

"But it *is* you," I countered reassuringly, "because it is your *natural*, right voice."

"It doesn't sound like me though . . . ," she said, her thoughts trailing off now in mild confusion.

She knew, somehow, that I was stating the truth. Her new voice worked better. It sounded better. Still, some part of her was resisting the change. That resistant force was her psyche, with whom I was actually carrying out this conversation.

Susan's psyche was comfortable with her habitual thin voice because it was a sound concept with which it was familiar. Hers was also a voice image that mirrored her self-image. By taking this first step, Susan had, without even realizing it, begun a quest for self-identity through her voice.

The proposal I made to Susan at the time is the same I now make to you: "Learn to use this new voice. Try it out. Perform a few voice exercises every morning. When you drive to work, read the street signs out loud as you pass them, trying to be aware of your correct pitch level. Think about tone focus so your sound will have resonance. Give breath support to your voice. And in the evening, spend a little time reading aloud from a book or from a newspaper. Record your progress on a tape player. When your initial anxiety about using a new voice has lessened, play back your tape and compare the difference between your old and new sounds. If, after a month or two, you wish to abandon your right voice, I'll know we've both tried. . . ."

Susan agreed this was a fair request. For the first few weeks, she used her new, natural voice only in the privacy of her own home or car and in my office. She did, however, practice the exercises and routines I'd prescribed.

Slowly, gradually, this new sound concept invaded her psyche, or so it seemed, because Susan began without conscious effort to use her right natural voice in conversation at work and with friends. After two months of therapy, she suddenly offered some good news.

"I think you're right," she said.

"About what?" I had my suspicions but wanted Susan to articulate her new voice consciousness.

"My voice," she answered enthusiastically. "It's making a difference. I noticed that people have started listening to what I say. They're being nicer to me for no reason at all. I think they must like my voice because nothing else about me has changed . . . which makes *me* feel better about myself."

Yes, perhaps Susan's co-workers and acquaintances did prefer Susan's new voice. More specifically, though, they were likely responding to the *dynamics* of her new voice. Her right sound was captivating and effective, where her old sound had been timid and thin. It was a pleasure to listen to her now, whereas before it had not been. She was, in effect, projecting a positive voice image, which generated positive reinforcement. As a result, Susan's self-image was improving. Her more positive self-image, in turn, shone through in her voice. Again, witness the circular, spiralling effects of voice usage, in this instance with rewarding consequences. In the end, Susan had acquired a commanding voice as well as greater self-esteem.

I have often observed in my patients that when you change a voice, you change a persona.

Kevin Warnecke is a young lawyer with the district attorney's office in Chicago. He had adopted a voice projected from the lower throat which he used as an intimidation factor. This is common among authority types. At our first meeting, he reported that his voice had begun failing him with increasing frequency. He was under a great deal of stress because of his vocal difficulties, and feared losing his job. He barked his complaints at me with a husky growl that was at best unpleasant and strained.

We quickly placed his voice in the mask and added tone focus and breath support. But Kevin fought this new voice because it was at odds with his voice image. "It sounds high and loud to me," he said bitterly.

I played back a recording of his right voice which revealed a baritone imbued with resonance. The voice was still deep, but the raspiness of his habitual sound had vanished. Kevin acknowledged that his new voice *was* neither high in pitch nor too loud. "It's not me, though," he repeated over and over. Then, finally, he offered of his own volition: "At least this voice works better than my regular voice, so I might as well give it a try."

In fact, this new voice was Kevin's physiologically correct sound. Over the course of a few months, it became his habitual voice. During this time I noticed some fascinating changes in Kevin which reflected not only an alteration of his voice image, but a marked difference in his manner, which I attributed to a more positive self-image.

The intimidation factor was removed from his voice and his presence. So was the edgy, apparent bitterness. He came across as competent and self-assured, instead of hostile and aggressive. I'll never know for certain if Kevin understood the change in his personality, though he did confide that his superior at the office had complimented him on his improved attitudes. "It's funny, don't you think," Kevin said, laughing, "that my boss thought I had a bad mental outlook when all I had was a bad voice. . . ."

Well, I'll let you draw your own conclusions from that one.

My purpose here is to impress upon you the role of voice images in your life. Your habitual voice was in all probability formed by societal influences that have nothing to do with your natural vocal abilities. Whatever the reasons for your voice type, whatever the extent of your current negative voice traits, you have a sound concept of yourself that your psyche might resist relinquishing. Furthermore, every psyche will manifest a different degree of resistance.

Authority types, such as Kevin, present the greatest

challenge. They have rigid expectations of themselves, as well as a rigid sense of what society expects of them. They are outer- *and* inner-directed to the extreme. Yet they adapt quickly to a new voice image once they observe that their natural right sound generates wider acceptance, socially as well as professionally.

More passive types tend to receive and use information with greater freedom and openness. Many make the transition to successful voice use very quickly. Others need gentle, constant encouragement. Susan, for example, risked putting herself on the line: Her shyness had impelled her to hide behind a weak voice all her life; abandoning this voice to a more dynamic sound meant exposing her true self to a world she feared yet longed to be a part of. The risk paid off.

The variables are impossible to predict, of course. Fay Williams has a strong personality, yet she completed her voice retraining in only two sessions. That's attributable to her determination to take charge of her own life.

Fay is an absolutely ebullient Englishwoman who came to America twenty-five years ago when she was a young starlet under contract to Metro-Goldwyn-Mayer. Her career never took off. When her contract expired, a studio executive told her that her blond good looks drew raves, that her acting ability was above average, but that her voice had a negative impact on audiences. She assumed he was referring to her English accent, and made a mental note to herself that Americans didn't like English accents.

Never mind. She was on to other things. Fay married, raised a family, opened a bookstore which did a healthy business. But as the years passed by, Fay was increasingly aware that people didn't like to talk to her.

Some people ignored her when she spoke. Some

physically moved away. She noticed that not a few people registered shock or displeasure on their faces the moment she began a sentence. Fay is a friendly, open person, and these rebuffs puzzled her. Then she came upon an article in which I discussed the ease of modifying accents. Remembering the incident with the studio executive, she vowed to at last rid herself of her communication handicap.

At our first session Fay told me in no uncertain terms that she had "had it with this English accent of mine. It will have to go. Will you help me?"

It was instantly apparent to me that her English accent was positively lovely. In addition, her voice was properly placed in the mask and had tone focus. Yet hers was a strident sound that had no appeal whatsoever.

Finally, lowering my volume as to test her hearing, I said, "Why are you yelling at me?"

"I'm not yelling," she responded with a force that caused me to feel I was bouncing off the wall. "This is my normal voice and I don't like it. I want to lose my accent, don't you understand?"

"But there is nothing wrong with your accent," I averred. "It's a classic."

"It's horrible," she hollered. "It's the reason no one likes me."

I asked Fay to decrease her volume by 50 percent, a request that perplexed her. But she did as I asked and the sound that emerged was pure music. Her voice was confident and sure but no longer overwhelming or strident. This softer tone quite simply put magic in all her inflections.

I had been recording our conversation, and I played back the tape so that she could hear the "before" and "after" voices. She acknowledged a notable difference but wasn't totally convinced her overbearing volume was the source of her problem. So Fay and I made a deal. I promised to help her alter her accent if, after two weeks, she was not happy with her new sound.

It took, in fact, only seven days for her to return with her verdict. "I'll never go back to that old voice again— this new sound is *great!*"

By decreasing her volume, Fay had solved a communication block that had plagued her for years, and which may have been largely responsible for curtailing her film career.

"My old voice *was* so loud that people found me irritating. At first it was difficult not to fall back into the old habits, but within a few days I could hear and control my volume. Now, people listen to me when I speak. They answer me when I ask a question. And they never turn and walk away from me the way they used to."

Amazing, isn't it, the impact an efficient, healthy sound can have? And in such a short span of time.

But Fay progressed so quickly because she was not afraid to try on a new voice image and test its results. And again, a new self-image emerged from the exercise. Because society "embraced" her new sound, so, too, did Fay. The outward approval of others instilled a sense of peace and self-acceptance within. Fay, English accent and all, had come home at last.

HEARING YOURSELF AS OTHERS DO

Since the bones in the head get in the way of your hearing your voice as others do, it's little wonder that you may never have had an accurate perception of your own sound. Hearing your voice played back on a tape recorder will give you a *sense* of how you really sound, but even here there are barriers which sometimes cloud the truth.

Many people initially find this such an unsettling experience that they actually refuse to believe that the voice they are hearing is their own. Distortion that doesn't exist is often imagined to be present. Excuses are often given in the form of, "This isn't how I normally sound. I'm tired today. . . ." Or cranky. Or depressed. Or nervous. Or excited.

In fact, it might be of some help to use a recording device during your voice retraining. You can start by making a short tape of your habitual voice when you commence the process. You don't have to listen to it. As you learn to use your right voice, add to the tape on occasion so that you will have a record of your progress. You will eventually find you have the courage to listen to and honestly appraise the changes in your sound.

In the interim, you can learn a great deal about yourself by listening to the people around you. You have the necessary information now to identify voice types, as well as their negative vocal traits. You can then apply the judgments you make about these sounds to what you wish to achieve or avoid in the use of your own voice.

Mary, for example, might produce her voice from the lower throat, causing it to be raspy and thus hard to understand or unpleasant to listen to. John might have a nasal sound which grates on your nerves. Tom might clear his throat several times in the course of a complex sentence, which proves distracting. And Jennifer might have a high, breathy sound which doesn't carry.

Do you wish to be perceived by others as you perceive these people? It only takes a bit of awareness of others and the negative voices they produce to cause you to tune in to your own vocal characteristics.

If you constantly clear your throat when talking, you know it by now. If you are constantly asked to repeat yourself, your voice is not well used. If callers ask to

speak to your mommy when you answer the phone (and
you happen to be forty years old), then your sound is not
serving you effectively. Does your voice fail you on occasion? Do listeners take a step backward when you
make small talk at a cocktail party? Do you know for
certain what sound will emerge when you open your
mouth to talk?

You are probably discovering without the aid of a
tape recorder that you do indeed know a lot about your
own voice and thus about the effect it must have on
others. Is it a sound you would like to listen to, day in,
day out? Maybe not, but there's still the question of that
voice image, deeply imbedded in your psyche, right?

Well, then, make a mental note of those who genuinely capture your full interest when they speak. My bet
is that they aren't squeaky or hoarse, that their voices
aren't breathy or strident or tightly controlled. In fact,
their voices are most likely so clear and natural and dynamic that you may never have been consciously aware
of their sounds. Instead, you have always been attuned
to their engaging personality traits or to the fascinating
content of their discourse. That's a sign of a well-used
voice *and* a positive voice image.

Now imagine that you too have a voice that enhances
rather than detracts from conversation, a sound that is
dynamic and natural rather than forced and phony. Keep
in mind that our purpose here is not to usurp another's
well-used voice but to discover your own and to use it
to equal advantage.

You will never, for example, sound like Johnny Carson, Orson Welles, or Rosalind Russell. And let's not
leave out Burt Reynolds. He's got much more than a
"pretty face"; he's got a terrific, properly produced
sound. Each of these celebrities uses the voice as a tool
for success. Note that each also has a distinctive sound,

unique to his or her own personality and physical ability. Your aim is to speak with a similarly effective voice that represents *your* best natural, unique self.

This would be a good time to repeat the exercises outlined in Chapter 2: a few "umm-hmmm's"; an instant voice press; some counting; a few energy words. "Hello. Right. Really. Beautiful." Be aware of a slight vibration in the mask, around the nose and mouth. Check to be sure you are giving your voice breath support.

As you gradually familiarize yourself with these simple mechanics, try, too, to familiarize yourself with your new personal sound concept. It belongs to you and you alone. It will, used over a period of time, become your new voice image, a successful reflection of your more positive self-image.

Visualize yourself in a social or professional encounter in which you are speaking with this, your right voice. The people about you are enticed by what you say because of the healthy dynamics that define your sound. Their attentiveness instills a warm feeling of confidence in you. You are becoming one with your sound; it is becoming one with you. Your former negative voice traits are fading from memory.

All that remains for you now is to actualize this vision.

TO FOLLOW THE LEADER—OR NOT

Even as your former voice image gradually becomes a thing of the past, replaced now by a successful, compelling voice image, you will continue to be bombarded by negative voice stereotypes throughout society. Since this is an inescapable phenomenon, how best can you protect yourself from these negative influences?

Firstly and most importantly, of course, is the fact of

knowledge. You know and understand a great deal more now about the correct use of your voice than you did previously. Because you are able to apply this information on a daily basis—both to the sounds you make and the sounds you receive—you will be much less likely to emulate others' misplaced voices than you were in the past.

In addition, you might even feel more healthy as a result of using your right voice. Most strain and anxiety formerly associated with voice use should have vanished soon after proper vocal technique was initiated. The physical and emotional rewards derived will give added impetus to make your correct, natural sound your habitual voice.

But there remains the pervasive influence of the electronic media. Here we are assaulted constantly with misused, abused voices presented through the often self-anointed form of "leaders." Besides actors, sports stars, weather forecasters, announcers, moderators, talk-show hosts, celebrity interviewees, we have above all our politicians and our news broadcasters who have achieved the exalted status of society's role models. They make the news and report it to us. With their power and prestige, it's little wonder they are often imitated by the public. But you'll find that the temptation to mimic them will be greatly reduced if you apply the same voice standards to these leaders that you now apply to yourself.

Keep in mind that media personalities are usually as ill-informed as the general society on the subject of voice production. And they are under even more intense pressure to conform to voice stereotypes. As authority figures, they tend to adopt the culture's conventional notion of an authority voice. The truth is, this tendency does not make them more effective leaders. It merely reveals that they are as vulnerable as everyone else to the prevailing myths and misconceptions about voice usage.

Most politicians fall victim to the myths the day they begin campaigning for election. They put on their leader's stance and their authority voice every time they go before an audience. The results are all too vivid and you need only turn on the evening news to hear them: Hoarse, cranky, forced, tired voices are given us as badges of relentless pursuit of the truth. I, for one, would prefer to hear the "truth" from a clear, intelligible, dynamic speaker.

The late President John F. Kennedy fell into this unnecessary pattern. Normally possessed of a fine voice —projected from the mask with balanced resonance— which he used in intimate or comfortably sized gatherings, Kennedy nonetheless forced his sound to the lower throat at times when campaigning. The evidence? Hoarseness after intense public speaking or debate. His brother, Senator Edward Kennedy of Massachusetts, does the same thing.

In election year 1976, former President Gerald Ford adopted an authoritarian pitch. I could hear the strain he was placing on his vocal mechanism and predicted he would lose his voice within a short period of time. Several months later, he did.

President Ronald Reagan was occasionally hoarse from voice misuse during the 1980 presidential race. But this is an aberration for President Reagan whose habitual voice is placed in the mask and enhanced by healthy tone focus. Notice that in most settings he speaks at a comfortable pace and tries to keep to subjects that interest him and about which he has a good working knowledge. This easy feeling is reflected in his voice. In all but rare instances, he keeps his tone personable, his style relaxed, using eye contact to sustain a rapport. It's not surprising that he is frequently mentioned in the press as a master communicator.

If you feel the need to single out one national leader who provides an example of successful, healthy voice use, President Reagan is a good choice.

One who stands out as a brilliant communicator is the late Dr. Martin Luther King, Jr. His magnificent voice—rich, full, well used in all its elements—gave urgency and forceful dynamism to his words. As Ron Hendren of NBC said in a 1983 commentary on the civil-rights martyr: "There hasn't been a leader . . . who knew so well what he wanted to say and how better to say it."

Such magical voices are few and far between, as you will be ever more aware. You won't want to follow the voice examples set by most poliltical leaders when, using the knowledge you have gained, you break down the components of their sounds to expose their lack of efficiency, intelligibility, clarity. You will happily reject, too, the sounds of most news commentators.

Men and women alike in this field force on themselves an authority voice that is not only boring and unappealing, but is in fact unhealthy. There is such a commonality of sound among them that it barely matters to whom you tune in each evening. Network upon network, night after night, you are likely to find the same colorless, undistinctive, flat reportage. And whom are most trying to imitate? The most famous broadcast journalist of them all, Walter Cronkite.

Walter Cronkite is the senior statesman of television news. He faithfully told us the way it was for years on end, and we, the viewers as well as his colleagues, came to trust and depend on him. It's not surprising then that those who wish to follow in his respected footsteps attempt to emulate him. The problem is, having set the standards for broadcast journalism, Walter Cronkite set one disastrous example among his other fine talents. Yes, that's right—I hate to burst the bubble, but in my professional judgment, Walter Cronkite has a troubled voice. It's forced, lacks carrying power, and has little versatility. This was not always so. The broadcaster formerly had a well-produced voice, projected from the mask. Unfortunately, he pushed his sound to the lower throat, ceased using his right, natural voice and in time came to serve as a wrong voice model for others.

To give perspective to this potentially upsetting revelation, I will tell you about a patient who was referred to me because he had completely lost his voice on numerous occasions. On those days when his voice did work, it was with great effort, often accompanied by pain. He had been forcing his voice from the lower throat and by now didn't know how to otherwise produce a voice. I asked him if he knew how or where he'd learned to speak like this.

"I dunno," he said with a rasp and a shrug.

"Does your father have a husky voice?" I inquired.

"No," whispered the patient.

"What about your mother? Or some other relative who has influenced your life? Or a teacher?"

He was terse: "No."

"I see. So you just sort of picked up this manner of talking, and it became your habitual voice?"

"Not exactly," he croaked hoarsely.

He cleared his throat and I sat patiently, waiting for him to elucidate.

"You see, when I grow up, I'm going to be Walter Cronkite," he said, at last. "I talk like him."

This patient was only eleven years old at the time and was already suffering the effects of voice abuse. His voice type could have been learned from many people in society, actually, but what's significant here is that this young boy had usurped the voice image of another in the misguided belief that he would then become like that person. Clearly, the voice image did not serve him well at all.

Today, young John Hastings has a clear, healthy, dynamic sound that is all his own. He has wisely chosen *not* to follow the leader, but to use the voice that nature intended him to have in the first place.

SEXUALLY SPEAKING

If your voice falls into the category of a "type," then you are by simple definition not presenting yourself in an individualistic manner. You are probably not using your right voice. But we have seen over and over again how readily, by dint of misinformation and/or cultural stereotypes, one can adopt a sound that is inappropriate.

Second only to the authority voice, the most commonly imitated and most inappropriate of society's voice types is the bedroom or sexy voice. This voice invariably manifests itself in limited volume, poor or nonexistent carrying power, a hoarse, husky, breathy tone, and a pitch level bordering on a low monotone.

I reiterate what I have previously told you: There is nothing wrong with a low voice. Rosalind Russell had a low-pitched voice. So, too, do Gregory Peck, Lorne Greene, Orson Welles. These low voices are not only acceptable but are dynamic because they are projected from the mask. There is, however, something terribly wrong with a voice that is projected from the lower throat—which is the source of sound in almost all of our culture's sexy or bedroom voices.

As described above, it should be quite clear that this voice type is not effective, is not versatile, is not healthy. It is not a successful sound because it interferes with communication. Why, then, do so many people adopt it as a voice image? Because the mass media have managed to persuade the public that *only* a voice produced from the lower one-third (of the throat) generates sex appeal.

If you have such a voice and endorse this mass-marketed concept, you may find it hard to shake your voice image. But your ability to overcome this vocal stereotype is strictly dependent on your willingness to embrace reality.

A well-used voice is as sexy a sound as you can find. Cary Grant *is* sex appeal. Burt Reynolds' career got launched on sexiness. Charles Boyer was long considered one of the sexiest stars in the world. Yet each is a perfect example of successful engaging vocal technique.

Brenda Vaccaro is a sexy actress with a voice projected from the lower throat. I dare you to assert that she would be less sexy if she learned to use her voice correctly.

Virginia English had a stereotypically sexy voice, too. And she liked being told her sound was sexy, so she never considered her recurrent hoarseness a handicap until it degenerated into constant laryngitis, the result of strain on the vocal mechanism. As a sales representative for a major toy company, she needed a functional voice. At our initial meeting, she said: "You turn on a faucet and you expect water to come out. Similarly, you open your mouth to speak and you expect sound to come out. I no longer have that luxury."

By this stage, her clients no longer wanted to hear her "sexy" sales pitch. As soon as they spotted her arrival, most raised their hands in a "sssshhh-ing" motion and encouraged her not to speak. They would be happy just to look at the catalog.

We corrected her pitch, added balanced tone focus

and midsection breath support. Her natural, right voice is lovely. It functions predictably now, both on the job and off.

"Ironically," Virginia says, "people still tell me I have a sexy voice."

Perhaps that's because she is a sexy woman?

VOICE PSYCHOTHERAPY

What we have been conducting in the preceding pages is a bit of voice psychotherapy. By demonstrating the pervasive influence of negative voice images—voice types that are frequently copied throughout society, as well as individual psychic adherence to a familiar sound concept—I have been hoping to instill in you a desire to liberate yourself and experience commanding and successful voice usage.

The change to a more positive and effective voice image will not likely be achieved unless your psyche is open to accepting such change. You must want to undo, modify, or resolve vocal characteristics that do not properly represent you. You must be prepared to resist societal influences that you will continue to meet in the form of negative or wrong voice models. You should not fear the reaction of others to your new right sound.

In fact, few, if any, people will actually be cognizant that your voice is different. As I've said before, most of us react negatively to distracting or unpleasant voices. We freely accept dynamic, healthy voices because such sounds allow for access to *content* (what is being said), as well as *personality* (who is saying it).

It does take time, patience, concentration to complete the transition to successful voice mechanics and positive voice image. So go easy on yourself, permitting relapses if they occur. But don't give up.

The ultimate gift you will give yourself is quality of voice, of presentation. Effective, compelling communication is worth the effort.

PACING YOURSELF

Most people find that it is easier to concentrate on the mechanics if they slow their rate of speech at the outset of the retraining process. Some do not require a slower pace. Since this is strictly an individual matter, you should experiment to see what works best for you. The key is to discover a rate of speech that enables you to be aware of content and the elements of voice simultaneously.

As you become increasingly familiar with your new sound concept, the elements of voice production will manifest themselves with greater and greater ease and spontaneity. When this begins to occur, you will want to establish a correct habitual rate of speech.

Personality variables and intellectual processes will to a great extent govern your pace of expression. If, for example, you have a quick mind that races on to new thoughts with excessive speed, you have probably incorporated this tendency in your speech patterns. You are likely to lose your listener's interest if your words and ideas run together.

So concentrate on enunciating each word and on completing each thought before introducing new notions into the conversation. Effective communication requires that you be heard and understood.

Conversely, you will bore your listeners if you speak too slowly. Do you pause between each word and each sentence? Do others put words into your mouth or complete thoughts for you? Do they try to hurry you along by interrupting and saying they know exactly what you're getting to? If so, you probably have too slow a rate of speech.

Actually, the mastery of the correct elements of voice usage will put more liveliness in your speech. This will generate greater interest from others. But you should still attempt to pick up your pace a bit. This can be easily accomplished.

Be aware of pauses when talking and eliminate some pauses except when needed for emphasis. Don't reach for abstract or sophisticated words unless they come naturally to you. Speak in simple, direct sentences using phrases that come immediately to mind. Again, the point is that you be heard and understood.

Rate of speech is a habit. Any and all habits can be modified if the individual desires and invites change. A more positive voice image—the result of correct voice production—is in and of itself a healthy habit that will instill confidence and assurance in your self-expression. Mastery of rate of speech should follow naturally now that you have made sound a compelling force in your life.

ASSOCIATE THERAPY

Here, again, you might feel the need for direct encouragement and reinforcement in achieving your aim. Are you still uncertain that yours is an effective rate of speech? Are you fearful or self-conscious when using your new, right voice in everyday situations? Do you simply require an opportunity to talk to someone about the changes you are undergoing? If so, a partner or associate can be beneficial to your progress.

As mentioned previously, it is often helpful to include a family member, a friend, or a colleague in the retraining process. You can monitor each other's progress and provide emotional support when needed. You can hear the changes in each other's sound better than you can hear the immediate change in your own sound. You are able to spot regression in an associate more readily than in yourself. A partner can alleviate any sense of isolation you feel as you gradually adopt a new voice and a better voice image.

CUES AND CATHARSIS

Most importantly, an associate who shares voice re-training with you can give you an outlet to discuss your anxieties, your fears, even your sense of excitement as you master the elements of voice usage. Dramatic change in life is almost always accompanied by some degree of stress. Even a new hair style is usually cause enough to give one the jitters. So don't be surprised if you experience nervousness as you begin to go "public" with your natural, right voice.

This is, in fact, a good sign because it suggests that this change in voice consciousness is more than a super-ficial alteration. It may even be that you are passing through a vocal identity crisis in which you are letting go of the old voice image—saying good-bye to a part of your past and accepting a new voice image. This can be temporarily traumatic for some people.

Some others will have a sense of abandoning a very real part of themselves. A voice, after all, *is* an aspect of self-identity. But if you have grown and changed, if you are no longer that streetwise kid from Brooklyn or that country-born-and-raised child from the Midwest, then perhaps the time *has* truly come to modify your voice to fit the new you. Yes, it can be an emotional moment when you realize you have transcended your origins or your former sense of self.

A partner or associate can give comfort and reassurance during such periods. You can do the same for him.

In time, you might each reach a point of vocal catharsis—a moment where you finally assimilate and embrace your new voice image. This, too, is an event to share.

As Barbara Collins, a teacher who successfully completed voice retraining, explained: "Integration of my new voice into *real life* was the hard part. But once this had occurred, I wanted to celebrate. . . . It had appeared to me in a flash of recognition, you see. And at first I became aghast that I had been allowed to grow up, then go to college and get a teaching credential with no training in the correct use of my voice. My voice, after all, is my primary instrument for conveying lessons. Then I realized, better later than never. And I suddenly understood that this new voice is my new reality. It's me as I am today. And I like it."

NOW REACH FOR THE BRASS RING

You're almost there. The gift of successful, vibrant communication can become *your* new reality, if you elect to make it so. The mechanics are easy to implement. Repetition and self-awareness will cause the mechanics to become second nature to you.

As this gradually occurs, you may experience a couple of common phenomena that you should be prepared for.

In the early stages of using your new, right voice, you might suspect that your sound has a singsong quality. Don't be disconcerted by this. What you are actually hearing is a new melodic and lilting inflection that results from the use of optimal pitch. It is a part of your new vocal dynamism and versatility. The exaggerated sense of this singsong quality will fade as you familiarize yourself with your new sound concept and establish a positive and compelling voice image.

You might also experience some physical changes which could include soreness along the neck; a tickling in and about the ear; a burning sensation in the soft palate. Such physical symptoms are no cause for alarm. They result, quite simply, from a realignment of muscles in the throat. The pressure lifts from the voice box and moves up to the jaw. These symptoms are comparable to the muscular soreness you experience when beginning a new exercise regime and should disappear within a few weeks, or even a few days. I tell my patients to think of this brief discomfort as an indication of vocal improvement unless, of course, they have *persistent* throat pain, hoarseness, or discomfort about the neck. Such symptoms are reason enough for a thorough medical examination.

You may also discover that your newly acquired breathing technique will create a trimmer midriff than you have ever had. Yes, midsection breath support gets the muscles in your midsection working correctly—as nature originally intended—which tones and firms the figure.

You will also note that your new voice works well even in noisy environments. You won't want to, or have to talk *above* or *below* loud sound because your breath support and tone focus will permit you to talk *into* it with ease.

These factors are all part of this new voice "technology"—a method of voice management and voice success that can and should present you to the world in a more compelling manner than ever before.

If you are willing to accept, practice, and enjoy the program I have described to you in these chapters, you can put voice magic into your sound, your psyche, your life! You may at last be blessed with that intangible power that commands attention and generates positive results. All you have to do now is reach for that brass ring—the vibrant "ring" of voice clarity, smoothness, efficiency, well-being.

PART TWO

Sound
and
(Voice)
Suicide

5

Why "Suicide"?

THE SOUNDS OF SILENCE

On certain days, those reserved for new patients, my office is one of the quietest places in town. In fact, if you were to place a blindfold over your eyes and be led (unknowingly) into my waiting room, you would perhaps believe yourself to be in some sort of sanctuary.

Lowering yourself onto the couch in this apparent den of tranquility, you would not feel alone, however. Doors would gently open and close. The soft rustling of movement would be heard as others enter, and then, in time, move to the inner sanctum—all without a word. Denied your visual perceptions, you might naturally conclude that you are in a monastery of some sort, perhaps amidst a sect that embraces the order of silence.

Letting your imagination take over, your mind's eye now envisions a gathering of cloaked figures, all immersed in quiet meditation. You wonder how it is possible, *if* it is possible, to live by choice without the advantage of speech. Contemplating the frequency with which you use your voice, you begin to squirm in your seat. These sounds of silence are disturbing for you know that you are not like these people in whose company you find yourself. Your curiosity building, you become anxious to see these transcendentalists, to observe them in their strange practice of quietude. Finally, pulling the blindfold away, you are confronted with—regular people. City people. Country people. A cross section of society, lacking the monastic garb you had mentally pictured.

Instead of monks, you find yourself among a teacher, a homemaker, a doctor, a lawyer. Present, too, is a rock'n' roll singer. Also an actress and a well-known entrepreneur. And a recognizable television announcer.

The announcer is wincing with pain; the lawyer is gesticulating in unsophisticated sign language to the doctor; the teacher is saving what is left of her voice for the brood of students she must soon confront. The rock'n' roll singer is possessed of no more than a raspy whisper. The homemaker sits in self-imposed quietude because her high-pitched, childlike mode of speech embarrasses her. As for the actress, she's lost two feature rolls in the past month because of a regional twang, and has sworn not to utter another sound in public until she corrects what has become an occupational liablity. For his part, the entrepreneur cannot speak. Try as he might, he is incapable of emitting a sound.

Dashed, now, are your illusions of this being a point of spiritual communing, though I hasten to add that I like to think of my office as a place of refuge.

And, having established that what all these patients have in common at this juncture of their lives is *silence,* the natural progression is to tell you why: Each has been committing one form or another of what I term *voice suicide,* the result of voice misuse and/or abuse.

Perhaps this expression sounds harsh to you. After all, the first part of this book dealt primarily with using your voice as a tool for success, which it can and should be. But I would be remiss in my duties if I didn't address myself to the potential consequences of long-term vocal misuse and abuse.

For as surely as a good voice can further you in life, a misused or abused voice can physically harm or impede you.

YOUR GOOD HEALTH IS AT STAKE

As I stated at the outset, I have spent the greater part of my career treating voice pathology. By the time most patients get to my office for consultation, they usually are suffering some type of serious vocal impairment that in the majority of cases could have been prevented by healthy voice technique.

Yet I continue, day after day, week after week, month after month, treating evergrowing numbers of defective voices. If you could see these patients, and hear their forced attempts to speak, you would instantly understand why I call them voice suicides.

While it is also true that I am treating more and more clients who simply wish to improve the quality of their voices, it is ever more apparent that a virtual epidemic of voice misuse and abuse exists in this country today.

My professional experience and clinical findings demonstrate that:

—At least 50 percent and probably more of the American population whose voices are considered "normal" have either aesthetically defective voices (nasal, whiny, raspy, thin, etc.), or episodic voice problems. These findings indicate misuse and abuse of the voice mechanism.

—From 10 to 25 percent could go on to develop one of many chronic voice conditions, and possibly pathology. This means that they are even now on their way to committing voice suicide.

—The resultant conditions of long-term voice abuse include nodes, polyps, and other growths on the vocal folds. Corrective measures include surgery and voice rehabilitation.

—Without proper treatment, benign growths on the vocal folds could end in premalignant conditions of the voice box, and possibly result in vocal fold cancer.

—If appropriate retraining of the voice is not completed following surgery, any of the above conditions might well recur, as further voice abuse causes increased physical impairment.

These devastating consequences of voice abuse can, however, be avoided or remedied by the use of correct vocal technique. And so, in Part Two of this book, we'll examine particular types of voice impairments, and discuss means of overcoming them.

Keep in mind that many medical doctors are only now catching on to the importance of healthy voice production. It's rarely discussed in medical school, so they have to find out on their own.

They, like you, are among the large percentage of the population that misuses the voice. They, like you, are among the countless committing voice suicide!

And what is worse is that much of what has been published by the "experts" in voice rehabilitation is theory that does not translate to practical success. Not only are the "experts" often wrong, but many of them are as vulnerable as you to the prevailing myths and misconceptions about the voice. They, too, suffer from misbegotten voice attitudes.

And yet the results I've achieved (and documented) prove that almost no voice deficiency (aesthetic or organic) is a serious problem to treat; in fact, almost all such disorders are functional in cause and respond positively to the correct voice techniques already outlined in Part One of this book.

Indeed, the results I've achieved prove that the attainment of a successful, natural, and healthy voice is so very simple—even if your vocal habits have already led you on a path to voice suicide.

UNDERSTANDING IS BELIEVING

Voice rehabilitation is a relatively new discipline which concerns itself with the production or "mis-production" of the speaking voice. As such, it focuses on the training or retraining of the voice to eliminate *dysphonias*. Dysphonia refers, simply, to any voice impairment or any difficulty in making voice sounds.

We alluded frequently to dysphonias in the preceding chapters by mentioning negative voice symptoms that interfere with communication. We attempted to show how and why these negative voice symptoms and images are begun and tolerated, both by the individual and the society at large. We also looked at the simple means with which the individual can rid himself of an ineffectual voice and achieve a dynamic, commanding voice. We did not, however, examine the dangers of perpetuating voice misuse and abuse.

Some readers may be shocked to learn of the disorders that can be caused by misuse of the voice mechanism. Others, who already suffer from serious vocal conditions, may be surprised to learn they are not alone.

To further explicate this whole issue of voice dysfunction, we'll have to get technical for a moment.

Organic dysphonias are voice disorders in which the larynx (or laryngeal structure) has been organically altered. In some instances, congenital or structural anomalies are at work (as in vocal fold paralysis); in others, partial or complete excision of the larynx is responsible, as might be required in the case of a primary disease such as cancer.

Most organic dysphonias, however, result from, or are perpetuated by, functional misuse or abuse of the voice. These include growths and lesions on the vocal folds, such as nodes and polyps, and contact ulcers. These conditions can be very serious, and require proper treatment.

In *functional dysphonias* there are no neurological or organic activating factors present. Voice misuse and/ or abuse is occurring within a normal laryngeal structure. Included in this group of disorders are spastic dysphonia; falsetto voice; nasality; and the largest category of defective voices—which I term "functional misphonias."

Functional misphonia is a specific term which actually means functional "wrong voice," a notion with which you are familiar. It defines a tired, hoarse, or weak voice, or one given to acute and chronic laryngitis.

It is this largest group, encompassing both functional misphonias and other functional dysphonias, that seldom, if ever, receives practical, sensible, or helpful treatment, and consequently can go on to involve more serious impairment. It is a spiralling movement, as increasingly greater numbers of patients end up in doctors'—and worse, surgeons'—offices, wondering why in the world they were never warned. They question, too, why their numbers are growing.

SOCIETY ENCOURAGES "WRONG" VOICES

Communication is the catchword of the eighties. It is as though, having emerged from the consciousness-raising reflection of the sixties, through the self-analytical and introspective seventies ("The Me Decade"), everyone is now anxious to talk. And the subjects open for discussion are countless.

People are talking about where they've been and what they've learned. They're talking about how they got where they are today, and what influences affected their decisions along the way. They're talking about the future, for themselves and their progeny. They're talking about sports and politics and the economy. They are communicating with a frenzy and intensity unmatched in days gone by.

They're doing it in all the traditional settings of human exchange. In schools, in courthouses, in the home, on the telephone. But in this revolutionary era of advanced telecommunications, people are also talking on big screens, on telephone answering machines, on cable networks, on sophisticated radio sets and before video cameras. Some people are already speaking to their computers. And as they use their voices more and more, they increasingly fall victim to the myths and misconceptions—the negative voice images—that prevail about voice production.

As we saw earlier, one of the most predominant of these myths is the American media's low-voice syndrome. This is a syndrome that began with the advent of "talkies."

You may know the story of John Gilbert, star and leading man of the silent films of his day. His great misfortune was the introduction of sound to film. His voice, high and squeaky and thoroughly unappealing by all accounts, was not at all consistent with his screen image. Blessed with a fine face and figure, revered as a screen hero, he was, nonetheless, ruined as a romantic lead because of his terrible voice. He fell from favor. As a result, voices all over America fell, too, to the lower throat.

Society had realized, in one stark moment, the importance of a good voice. John Gilbert's example, though, inspired the belief that a high-pitched voice was a bad voice, and thus, that a low-pitched voice was a good voice. The genesis of what would become a veritable epidemic had taken root.

In fact, John Gilbert could no doubt have improved his sound and continued his career—if only someone had been around to teach him to produce his natural and right voice from the mask.

But from that time forward, a low, throaty tone was *de rigueur.* This syndrome is still so prevalent that people adopt it as a matter of course, forcing their voices to the lower throat intermittently, and in some cases, permanently. Voice coaches, speech teachers, and clinicians (most of them trained in articulation, not voice production) encouraged the low voice. Lawyers, teachers, physicians, politicians, secretaries, executives, parents, were encouraged to use it. The media adopted it as a norm. And so America as a whole embraced this low-pitched voice as a model, a voice image to be emulated.

This is the basal pitch used by Henry Kissinger. It was employed, too, by O. J. Simpson during Monday night football broadcasts in the fall of 1983. Before he sought my help, sports columnists and fans had complained about a lack of intelligibility, a lack of carrying power in his voice. Individuals who use this voice often find that others cannot understand them even when they are in a quiet environment.

But those who use the basal pitch consistently, and who attempt to add volume to it, manifest more obvious problems and may suffer even greater disabilities. You must have noticed, for example, how frequently newscasters (most of whom speak from the lower one-third), clear their throats without relief during their broadcasts? Or, how often politicians in the throes of campaigning become hoarse or lose their voices altogether?

These symptoms result from misusing and abusing

the vocal apparatus. In other words, from forcing a sound that is not natural to the physiological abilities of the voice mechanism. While the use of such a voice does not always incapacitate the individual, it at best reduces fluidity and effectiveness of communicating. And it often does worse.

Many years ago, I was interviewed by a well-known Los Angeles talk-show host. He listened politely to my views about voice production and then challenged me to analyze his voice.

I respectfully warned that speaking from the lower throat, as he did, was dangerous. I suggested he raise his voice to the mask. He rejected this proposal.

Nine years later, this same talk-show host sought my help in overcoming hoarseness, regularly recurring voice loss, and severe pain about the larynx. This pain, coupled with an inability to perform his on-air job, suddenly became a forceful motivation to acquire proper voice use. Using the same techniques now known to you, these problems were quickly resolved.

The basal pitch level which the TV personality had been using is responsible for most dysphonias. And as you and your friends and your colleagues and your relatives use it more and more—as part of the communication decade of the century—growing numbers of you might find yourselves seeking help and wondering how you went wrong. Unless, that is, you recognize your own symptoms of voice misuse and abuse and correct them.

YOUR BODY IS TRYING TO TELL YOU SOMETHING

Most of us learn early in life to recognize negative symptoms when they present themselves. Abdominal pain, nausea, or dizziness, for example, are instantly interpreted as signs of physical distress. Such distress might represent, respectively, appendicitis, food poisoning, or inner-ear disturbance. We have been taught, by society or by our parents, that the correct and appropriate response to such occurrences is to seek treatment.

Treatment for voice distress, however, is rarely sought. This is because most people never have been taught to recognize the symptoms of vocal impairment. Despite pain about the larynx or dysfunction, defective voices are generally tolerated with casual resignation. Yet negative voice symptoms are every bit as significant as abdominal pain or vertigo.

These symptoms present themselves as signs of physical distress. They indicate that your body is trying to tell you something—that is, that corrective measures are required because something is wrong.

Once you know what they are, most negative voice symptoms of functional and organic dysphonias are easy to spot in yourself. Sensory symptoms are those felt by you; auditory symptoms are those heard by you and by listeners; visual symptoms are those seen by a medical doctor.

Visual symptoms are determined by a laryngoscopic examination. If symptoms are present, the vocal folds might reveal redness, inflammation, or swelling. Diagnosed disorders could include thickening of the vocal folds; growths or lesions on the vocal folds; bowed vocal folds; a paralyzed vocal fold; and possible neurological involvement.

If you are suffering any of these conditions because of voice misuse, you will most likely already be experiencing either sensory or auditory symptoms, or both.

The *sensory symptoms* include nonproductive throat clearing; coughing; progressive voice fatigue following brief or extended voice use; acute or chronic irritation or pain in or about the larynx; swelling of veins and/or arteries of the neck; throat stiffness; feeling of a foreign substance or a lump in the throat; ear irritation or tickling; repeated sore throats; scratchy or dry throat; a feeling that talking is an effort; a choking feeling; tension and/or tightness in the throat; earache; back-neck tension; headache; mucus formation; pain at the base of the tongue; and chronic toothache without apparent cause.

The most common sensory symptoms are voice fatigue, coughing, and throat clearing. Unfortunately, these negative tendencies are considered normal, so they go unacknowledged as signs of voice misuse or abuse. You may, in fact, have experienced such symptoms for such an extended period of time that you have become insensitive to the discomfort or pain caused by them.

I interviewed a new patient recently who cleared his throat fifteen times in the first three minutes of our discussion. He was completely oblivious of this habit, though he was complaining of periodic voice problems.

When the voice is misused, actually, nature protects and soothes the vocal cords by releasing a flow of mucus over the vocal fold, which is fine except that now the mucus must be expelled so as not to interfere with speech. So the throat is cleared. But continued voice abuse persists in squeezing the voice box, and the gland under the vocal fold releases more mucus. Again the throat is cleared. The cycle is perpetuated until only coughing succeeds in clearing the mucus. This, in turn, further irritates the vocal mechanism. It's no wonder the voice grows tired.

But curiously, you probably accept voice fatigue as a natural function of voice use.

I tell you now in no uncertain terms that a properly produced voice should not tire or lose volume or intelligibility however much it is used, except in circumstances that interfere with proper voice usage—such as extreme mental or physical exhaustion, emotional trauma, or the type of severe cold caused by a virus that attacks the vocal folds.

Otherwise, under normal conditions, correct voice usage should prevail.

A well-produced voice flows smoothly, constantly, at the right pitch, with tone focus and resonance (and hypnotic effect), for any length of time, and this means without voice fatigue, throat clearing, or coughing. Keep in mind that constant screaming at ballgames or in routine competition with loud noise *can* damage the voice box!

Yet you not only *feel* your own negative voice symptoms, but you *hear* them, in yourself and others, and you perceive them or accept them as "natural," or "normal."

Auditory symptoms include acute or chronic hoarseness; reduced or limited vocal range; inability to talk at will and at length in variable situations; tone change from a clear voice to a breathy, raspy, squeaky, froggy, or rough voice; repeated loss of voice; laryngitis; voice breaks, voice skips; a voice which comes and goes during the day or over a period of months; clear voice in the morning with tired or froggy voice in the afternoon or evening; missed or inaudible speech sounds.

The most common auditory negative voice symptom is hoarseness. It is prolonged and often painful hoarseness that finally brings many patients to the physician and, ultimately, to my office.

WHY NO ONE EVER TOLD YOU BEFORE

We spoke at length in the first half of this book about using the voice as a tool for success. Since we all require a voice to aid us in communication, it might as well be a good, indeed a commanding, voice. But some readers may still be finding it hard to accept the darker, more threatening aspect of voice misuse: The symptoms listed above could result from incorrect voice usage.

Others, who have sought help for such symptoms but who have not found success from medical intervention, may by now be awakening to the realities of voice use, misuse, abuse. But the question that must be presented time and again through this discourse is: Why hasn't anyone told me these things before?

The fact is that physicians all too often know as little as the layman on the subject of voice production. Medical institutions do not train them in this area. And thus, because precipitating factors of serious voice disorders are often misunderstood, many patients find themselves making the "medical rounds," referred from one specialist to another. Most get discouraged as a result of the conflicting medical opinions hurled at them. Many become depressed and increasingly isolated. It can be distressing, going through life without a voice, or without a voice that you can count on to work when you need it.

Helen Borson suffered this fate.

Her voice went hoarse for the first time in 1972, while she and her husband were on vacation. She attributed the problem to "overuse" of her voice and thought little more of it. But as time went on, her hoarseness began recurring with increasing frequency.

Meanwhile, Helen's husband was complaining that he couldn't hear her well when she spoke. He often had to ask her to repeat herself. Though he wasn't having the same problem with others, he allowed Helen to convince him that something was wrong with his hearing. He went to a specialist, who found no defect. Still, no one suggested that Helen's voice might be deficient.

Finally, however, Helen's voice became constantly

hoarse. At about the same time, she happened to hear an old recording of herself speaking. She compared the difference—before the hoarseness and after—and became alarmed. Her father, it seems, had died of throat cancer and the symptoms were all too familiar to Helen. She decided she needed help.

In 1981, Helen consulted with three ear-nose-throat doctors. X-rays were taken of her sinus cavities, of her ears, of her nose, of her throat. No cause could be found for her hoarseness. Her internist eventually suggested the possibility of allergies as the root of her problems. The allergist who tested her found nothing. And so, in time, Helen checked herself into a famous medical center in California for a complete physical examination. There she was told for the first time that there were irregularities about her vocal cords. The suggested solution? To stop talking.

Another consultation with yet another medical specialist confirmed irritation of the vocal cords. Now, at last, a well-informed doctor told Helen she was misusing her voice. Since she had never before heard such a concept, Helen was uncertain as to her next step.

A chance meeting with an old friend who had suffered a similar ordeal resulted in a referral to my office. Like so many other patients, Helen found it hard to believe that her negative symptoms could be so quickly analyzed and readily solved. She had simply to learn to produce her voice from the mask, and to provide midsection breath support.

Her voice had "bottomed out," I explained. She habitually spoke from the lower throat, with a basal pitch, and that was the reason others had difficulty understanding her. This basal pitch, used over years, had caused vocal fold irritation, which had, in turn, resulted in a hoarse, froggy voice.

"Why," she finally said, "didn't anyone ever tell me these things before?"

It is a question asked often of me. And of course the only possible answer is that too many physicians and speech therapists have not had relevant training which enables them to understand the speaking voice. They, like the beleaguered patient, search for a complex explanation and an even more complex solution to problems that are really quite straightforward.

So again and again, I go back to the simple, direct elements of correct voice production, applying these basics to patients who suffer from severe dysfunction as well as to clients possessed only of a desire to improve the aesthetics of their voices. The fundamentals consistently provide the key to success.

It's a success that can be yours.

True, your own bad voice habits—not to mention your negative voice symptoms—may not have incapacitated you, *yet.* But without even knowing it, you might be among the many who continuously misuse the voice, until, one day, it finally will break down from the abuse.

WHERE DO YOU STAND NOW?

If you are among the many who have already decided to incorporate the elements of healthy and successful voice techniques into your lives, you may not need to read on. By now, in fact, many readers may have effectively mastered these elements and acquired a new and commanding sound, as well as a more compelling voice image. But if you or your friends or relatives are still manifesting negative voice symptoms, you may want to be aware of the stages of symptomotology. This will enable you to see more clearly how seemingly benign tendencies can turn into serious and threatening symptoms when ignored, as they usually are in our society.

The negative symptoms of voice misuse and abuse occur in three stages. They range from mild to severe. They may be sensory (those we can feel), auditory (those we can hear), or visual (those that can be detected by laryngoscopic examination). One or more symptoms may be experienced in each grouping.

The First Stage: Sensory: slight pain or irritation after prolonged voice usage; some tension in or about the larynx; mild mucus flow; some scratchy or itchy sensation within the larynx; infrequent throat clearing; an occasional sore throat. Auditory: slight hoarseness; mild laryngitis; some reduction in carrying power; thinning of voice as the day progresses; some restriction in voice range. Visual: inflammation or redness of vocal folds.

The Second Stage. Sensory: frequent throat clearing; increased tension in or about the larynx; irritation of the larynx; periodic sore throat; a feeling that speech is an effort; voice fatigue after fairly brief voice usage. Auditory: moderate hoarseness; some voice breaks or skips; periodic laryngitis; reduced voice range; episodic loss of voice; more pronounced vocal impairment through the day. Visual: thickened or swollen vocal folds; incipient (beginning) vocal nodules, polyps, or contact ulcers; slight bowing of the vocal folds.

The Third Stage. Sensory: quick voice fatigue after brief voice usage; a feeling of a foreign substance or lump in the throat; consistent nonproductive throat clearing; strained speech; irritation or pain about the larynx; excessive mucus flow; recurrent sore throat; rumble in the chest; severe tension in the throat. Auditory: recurrent hoarseness and/or laryngitis; repeated voice breaks and skips; marked reduction in voice range; repeated loss of voice; noticeable difficulty in being understood; evident lack of carrying power; voice failure occurring earlier in the day. Visual: growths or lesions on the vocal folds; pronounced bowing of the vocal folds; paralyzed vocal fold.

All the stages described do not occur in each individual. Some stages progress more rapidly than others, with individual variation, and some stages remain static in certain people.

By now you are aware of your own negative voice symptoms, as well as the stage of distress they fall into. Let's get a clearer idea of what can happen if you choose to ignore these symptoms.

A NOT UNCOMMON STORY

Serious voice impairment usually occurs after many years of voice misuse and abuse. It is for this reason that such disorders seem to appear more often in adults than in children. In fact, voice patterns, good or bad, often begin at an early age, particularly those patterns that pertain to regional or familial influences.

New Yorkers and Midwesterners alike share a tendency for nasal tones (voices placed in the upper one-third). Southerners are known for their slow and easy drawls, though there are geographical distinctions among them. New Englanders tend to have a clipped manner of speaking.

All these voices are a product of environment, not heredity. They are voice types that are described by regional phonations or aesthetic qualities. Some people like them. Others do not. Singly, without abusive inclinations, they will not cause harm. They can be changed and modified if the individual so wishes, to soften or discard accents, or to improve vocal quality or voice effectiveness.

Other voice types, however, demand voice retraining. The case, and voice type, of Barton Cummings provides one such example. His story is not an uncommon one.

Barton's voice was characterized by a basal pitch, in the lower one-third, and used as an authority voice. It is impossible to guess when or why he began pushing his voice to the lower throat, as even he had no distinct recollection.

Sometimes this tendency begins with no more than a cold, which causes the voice to take on husky tones. With or without conscious effort, these tones can be carried on in normal speech after the cold has passed. The same can happen with early morning voice raspiness that many people have upon awakening. Prolonged exposure to excessive air conditioning can instill this voice pattern.

So, too, can trauma. Shock or distress or profound disappointment frequently result in low or somber tones which are then incorporated as a continuing habit.

Barton could not recall such an incident, or a specific onset of low-voice syndrome, but then he had never even been aware of making a change to it.

Certainly, he said, he'd had no negative symptomatology during his years as a reporter for the *New York Times*. But during those years he had not had to use his voice extensively—only in normal conversation and interviews. He had spent a good part of each day writing his column and "resting" his voice.

But then he began a series of occupational changes —from reporter to film studio executive to movie producer—that gave him little opportunity to limit the use of his voice. As vice-president in charge of production for Paramount Studios, which averaged forty pictures a year during his tenure, he found himself engrossed in conversation during all of the twelve hours he worked each day. There were telephone calls with agents, meetings with directors, readings with actors, discussions with studio officers. There were business lunches and business dinners.

His voice began to thin, or wear out, during the course of the day. By evening, he sometimes had a sore throat.

His symptoms progressed as time went on. At age thirty-six, Barton was experiencing voice fatigue by midday. He had to clear his throat frequently, which only seemed to aggravate the soreness about his larynx. He attributed these "minor" problems to overuse of his voice and to the stress of his job. He began using throat lozenges and cough syrup. This palliative course seemed to ease temporarily the irritation he felt about his lower throat.

In the next few months, the studio executive was suffering voice fatigue earlier in the day. By now he was consistently clearing his throat. Talking was a chore. Because others had difficulty hearing him clearly over the phone, he had to strain for volume. Eventually, he would have to install a voice amplifier on his telephone.

He was finally becoming worried about his now constant hoarseness, but his friends and co-workers insisted it was a great sound. He had a "sexy" voice, they said.

And then persistent laryngitis set in. By the time he finally saw a throat specialist, Barton's misuse and abuse of his voice had resulted in nodes and lesions on the vocal folds. He had barely a voice at all when he entered the hospital for surgery. His operation and two-day hospital stay cost him and his insurance company thousands of dollars. All this because he had never been taught to properly produce a voice!

And there was an additional price to pay: the imposition of complete silence during the four-week healing period after surgery. Then, of course, he had to undergo voice retraining.

Barton was taught—as are all my patients—to project his voice from the mask, to achieve oral-nasal resonance, and to provide his voice with midsection breath support. I should emphasize that his voice retained its deep sound (yes, it still reflected authority!), but now it was a better, more commanding voice. By the time he was thirty-eight, Barton's voice was healthy.

The nodes and lesions on his vocal cords have not recurred, thanks to his continued use of proper voice techniques.

TOO MANY STORIES TO RECOUNT

People often accuse me of being an alarmist. I talk and write about voice suicide. I travel the country lecturing about healthy voice projection from the mask. I am frequently invited to address professional groups and local workshops on the subject of voice techniques. I have appeared on television shows and been interviewed on radio.

These forums give me the opportunity to disseminate information that has not been previously available to most people. Yes, I tell my listeners, you *can* improve the quality and effectiveness of your voice by learning to use it properly. No, I repeat over and over, you are *not* stuck forever with this sound that you have always thought of as your natural voice—because it probably isn't the voice nature intended you to have. The magic, I repeat over and over, is in the mask.

Yet time and again I get back to the subject of voice abuse and its potential consequences. And so perhaps I *am* an alarmist. I just can't seem to stick with the good

news, that you can become better than you are, that a
key element of success is in the voice. I always move on
to the bad news—the warnings, the hazards, the health
factors. And for good reason.

The fact is a large percentage of the American popu-
lace is hurting itself through improper voice technique.
I've seen and treated too many Helen Borsons, heard
the tales too many times of making the rounds from one
medical specialist to another without relief. Too many
Barton Cummings fail to realize they're in trouble until,
suddenly, they find themselves entering a hospital for
surgery that might have been prevented. If only they'd
known.

"If only I'd known. . . ." That's what Gary Johnson
said after a few therapy sessions in my office in 1972.

Gary was one whose voice went out quickly and
without warning for the first time in 1967. As a successful
construction manager, Gary often had to compete with
very loud environments when visiting building sites.
But he'd never had problems with his voice before as a
result of forcing volume. Now, though, within the span
of a week, his voice had become so hoarse he could
barely utter a sound.

His doctor diagnosed a growth on his vocal fold that
would have to be surgically removed. The procedure
was performed, and Gary thought his troubles were
over. Actually, they were just beginning.

The growth returned again and again. In the period
of two years following the onset of his hoarseness, Gary
Johnson had the same operation five separate times. Despite the recurrence of his malady, no one ever suggested a *cause*, or, for that matter, a preventive measure.

Finally, in 1972, a biopsy of yet another growth on
his vocal fold revealed papilomatosis, a precancerous
condition. Though frightened by this news, Gary was by

now determined to find a nonsurgical solution. A series of professional consultations led him to me, and we began treatment to correct his voice misuse and abuse. His voice retraining lasted approximately one year. During that time, the growth on his vocal fold receded, then resolved. He learned to place his bass-baritone voice in the mask and to buttress it with breath support from the midsection.

Ten years passed before I heard from Gary Johnson again. In 1983, while visiting Los Angeles from Atlanta, he came to see me. Neither the growth nor the precancerous condition had recurred during that time. His right, natural voice had worked just fine for him in all the years since his therapy. Our meeting was brief, but filled with warm appreciation on his part for the information and retraining I'd given him.

There are so many stories like this in my files. Stories such as Helen's, Barton's, Gary's. Too many to recount. I hope they serve to explain why I talk and write about voice suicide. Why I want to warn my audiences and my readers about the hazards of vocal abuse. Why I wish to share with them the tools for healthy voice production.

DON'T BE A LOSER, BE A WINNER

There are many of you, and you know who you are, who have long been looking for solutions to voice problems. Whatever your form of voice distress, the tools for healthy communication can now become yours. Perhaps you suffer from a stutter? Well, we'll discuss this problem shortly. Or, maybe you are among those who are, quite literally, terrorized by spastic dysphonia. We'll soon take a look at this most confounding disorder.

As I have said so often in the course of this book, the fundamental elements of voice production always apply.

Your voice can be better than it is. The decision to make it so is up to you.

Winston Churchill decided to overcome his handicap. He chose to be a winner, not a loser. And so can you. Try it. You might like it.

6

Special Problems

Though the voice is used for up to 80 percent of all communication, voice use is seldom if ever referred to in society as either a tool for achieving success or for maintaining good health. In the first part of this book we at last broke through the wall of silence on this subject and introduced the concept of voice magic. We examined and dissected the various ways in which a good voice can serve the individual by presenting him to the world in a dynamic and compelling manner. We described the mechanics of correct voice usage, and how to achieve them. And we looked at voice models—both positive and negative—and showed how they can help or hurt us.

Along the way, abbreviated case histories of former patients were used to illustrate the unfortunate impact of poorly used voices, as well as the sense of well-being that is derived from correct voice technique. The patients mentioned all had some negative voice trait or physical symptom that finally necessitated help being sought. Each had a physical complaint or sound deficiency that got in the way of effective communication. Most readers will have been able to identify their own voice defects from the case histories presented. And they most certainly now understand the benefits to be gained by employing proper voice technique.

Others, however, may still feel isolated and even a bit desperate, for they suffer from advanced voice disorders that are truly incapacitating. These are the voice suicides who, like Helen, Barton, and Gary are in some manner immobilized by their conditions.

They are the people who stutter uncontrollably. Or who produce grotesque sounds when they attempt to talk. Or who do not know from moment to moment if they have a functioning voice. Or who can't risk answering their own telephones because they fear being ridiculed or misunderstood.

Such victims are cut off from the normal gossip, quips, sharing of information and life stories and anecdotes that most of us enjoy on a daily basis. What's worse, they tend to feel completely alone in the world, unaware that others share their dreadful fate. There is, at least, *some* consolation in exchanging tales of woe. But how can one find a partner in misery if one is incapable of talking or too terrified to try?

To add to their troubles, a great proportion of voice suicides have been told to search for a psychiatric cure. The assumption here is that where a medical solution cannot be found to heal their voice ills, there remains only a psychological cause to be unravelled in prolonged therapy. This type of thinking leaves the victim not only without a voice, but with the frightening sense that he or she is emotionally unbalanced.

While I have seen many patients emerge from psychiatric counseling with great insights into themselves and their motivations, I have seen very few voice disorders overcome solely as a result of such therapy. This is an expensive, experimental, circuitous route to voice health, at best.

Meanwhile, jobs are lost and family members grow impatient.

I treated a teacher from Florida whose school board blamed her voice loss on her subconscious desire to give up working. Psychiatric care was begun to confirm this charge. In fact, her vocal difficulties had appeared after extended exposure to the excessively cold air conditioning in her classroom which pushed her voice to the lower throat. In turn, this now-habitual voice pattern strained the vocal mechanism which caused her voice to go out completely. Neither the teacher nor her school board had ever heard of voice misuse. Nor, unfortunately, had her psychiatrist.

Another patient, an insurance salesman from North Dakota, had not had a conversation with his wife in the entire two years before he came in for his first consultation. "It just drives her crazy when I try to talk," he rasped forth in a guttural sound with skips and breaks that obscured much of what he said. "I guess she thinks I can get better if I want to. But I don't know how. So what's the use in trying anymore?" Not only had this man lost his job, but now he had effectively lost his confidante, the wife who had been his partner in life for twenty-five years.

Such sad tales are not as unusual as you might think. But one doesn't run into these people very often in regular society. That's because, when efforts at communication at last prove exhausting, humiliating, and futile, voice suicides withdraw, further isolating themselves from a world that seems to offer no aid or comfort.

Both the teacher and insurance salesman had lost their vocal ability after being established in careers. Each now anticipated major adjustments in professional goals as well as in their interpersonal relationships. Others, whose voice dysfunction begins earlier in life, quite literally plan their futures to accommodate their voice disorders.

A young woman who had stuttered since the age of five became a botanist because "plants don't seem to care if you're verbally handicapped." She would rather, she confessed, have become a doctor. "But doctors have to talk to people." It took her a full sixty seconds to articulate this simple sentence.

A young man who had had "a terrible-sounding voice my whole life" elected to become a writer in the field of educational research. A career in which he dealt with the written word rather than the spoken word would insulate him from people who had "always reacted negatively to me when I spoke," he said. The mere act of talking had always been a physical effort for him. He had frequently been asked to repeat himself throughout his childhood, his adolescence, his college years. And his voice frequently failed to work at all. His voice problems had been attributed to allergies.

"But I developed peripheral mannerisms that I can trace directly to my vocal difficulties," he explained. "I began mumbling when I was a kid. And I acted aloof, pretending I wasn't interested in others. I wanted to reject them before they rejected me."

But he encountered one problem he hadn't planned for: He was a gifted writer who became an expert in his field. His professional peers wanted to meet him and discuss his work. "It was horrendous. I could tell they were put off by my voice. As soon as they got the basic information, they would leave the room or hang up the phone. I felt more alone and more dejected than ever."

This sense of loneliness is common among those who have experienced serious voice impairment. If you are one of the countless in this group of voice suicides, you needn't feel alone anymore.

Yes, that's right, there's help for you, too.

Like the teacher, the insurance salesman, the botanist, the writer, you can discover the rewards of healthy, successful communication. You can rejoin society, confident of having a well-functioning voice. You will use the same methods of voice retraining described earlier in this book. But you will have added insights to get you on your way.

As for the teacher, several months of functional voice retraining brought back the voice that two years of analysis had failed to resurrect. The insurance salesman recovered his voice, too. And the botanist ceased stuttering. The writer learned to use his right, natural voice and felt at ease with himself and the world for the first time in his life.

"It's gratifying now to talk to people," he told me at our final session. "The quality of conversation is so improved. The content is the same, actually. But it goes further, to the point where I have real relationships."

And then he confided the following to me: "I had a dream, a conscious dream, about a year ago. I decided to fantasize about the best possible life I could have. I wished for a better job, one that wasn't so isolated. I wished I could be more socially alive. And I wished for a better voice to allow it all to happen."

By now the young researcher had a good, healthy voice. His sound came from the mask, complemented by balanced tone focus. He still discreetly monitored his breathing occasionally while talking by simply placing one hand on his midsection to insure correct breathing technique.

Six months later, I received a telephone call from this man who had formerly spoken only through his writing. His new job was very rewarding, he reported. He spent only half his time in research and writing now, and the other half traveling and lecturing. "Public speaking is easier than I ever thought possible," he said in a full, rich, natural voice.

ANXIETY AND FEAR IN COMMUNICATION

The young man described above was afraid of verbal communication most of his life. As a consequence he avoided it. Once he had mastered the basic elements of voice usage, however, a whole new world opened up to him. He was confident enough to accept a new job that brought him out of the "laboratory" whose insulation he had long coveted and insisted upon. He was courageous enough to attempt public speaking by which he would formerly have been mortified. Yet he was actually enjoying it. Having a voice—his right, natural voice—gave new meaning to his life. He was finally an active participant.

Note that his voice dysfunction was not caused by a fear of communication; rather, his fear of verbal communication was caused by his voice dysfunction. This is frequently the case among voice suicides and is verifiable by the fact that once they are possessed of a functional voice—especially one that serves them well—fear and anxiety in vocal expression seems to completely vanish.

This is the reason that I stress the basics of voice production in management of voice disorders. I normally find that whatever psychological factors and stresses are said to be present, it is the voice misuse and abuse that cause the voice dysfunction. And whatever the precipitating circumstance—a wrong voice model, a cold, trauma, exposure to excessive air conditioning—it is the lack of voice training that allows voice misuse to be perpetuated.

Once a wrong voice has been established and used long enough to produce negative results, emotions and tensions can and do aggravate both the voice disorder and the psyche. And so it is that the voice retraining and voice psychotherapy are carried out simultaneously. Wrong voice models must be eradicated at the same time the wrong voice is being shed. By the time the right voice has been identified and achieved as a habitual sound, the psyche is ready and able to accommodate a new sound concept. Here we have a successful transition from negative habitual voice to positive new voice image.

Notice that in *voice* psychotherapy, it is *vocal neuroses* that are discussed and modified. No mention is made of deep-rooted or other psychological neuroses because their possible existence does not seem to inhibit the *functional* use or retraining of the voice. My role as voice therapist is to aid the patient in achieving a functional right voice—a dependable, clear, and dynamic sound—in the most straightforward and direct manner possible. And so we do.

But there are exceptions to every generalization, of course. Fear and anxiety *do* enter as causal factors in two of the most troubling disorders, spastic dysphonia and stuttering, but with curious twists.

Spastic dysphonia is often called a "monster voice." This is because the sounds that emerge from its victims are quite truly monstrous: strained, broken, forced, guttural. As you will soon see, life itself becomes terrifying for individuals who suffer from this dysfunction. So it's not surprising that their initial fears and anxieties escalate and further torment these individuals.

Stuttering is a more familiar stigma to the general

society. Manifesting itself as a forced, labored stumble in speech, or as an abnormal, rapid repetition of certain sounds, this condition is viewed with derision, mockery, and avoidance by those with "normal" speech patterns.

In fact, the stutterer is not a foolish, weak, or flawed person. Why, then, does he (or she) sound as he does? Because he has a more perfectionist leaning. . . .

STOP STUTTERING NOW

While stutterers suffer form the same dearth of knowledge about voice usage as the rest of our society —resulting in misplaced pitch, lack of tone focus, incorrect breathing technique, and wrong voice models— most have a misconception about speech patterns that sets them apart from the rest of us in their verbal expression.

They believe that speech should be perfect. And this is where fear and anxiety come into play in the majority of stuttering problems. The anxiety that attends the desire to create perfect speech instills a fear of failure to do so, which in turns creates *im*perfect speech. It's a classic example of a self-fulfilling prophecy. But it's a prophecy that recurs over and over again in the life of a stutterer, plunging the victim ever deeper into the abyss of his speech habits. Still, he tries even harder to force a perfect speech image and fails. He begins to develop a fear of certain sounds, such as a "th" sound, or an "s" sound. And now he starts anticipating these sounds when he talks and tries to preform them by placing the tongue against the back of the teeth or pressed hard in the roof of his mouth. He cannot talk when his tongue is stiff, of course, so more dysfluencies occur. By now, the habitual speach is filled with machine-gun repetitions or drawn-out stumbles. And sometimes distracting body postures are taken on because of these difficulties in communicating, adding to both physical and mental tension and exacerbating the fear and anxiety.

Stutterers, led for the most part by false images and wrong illusions about effective communication, do not understand or accept what most of us blithely take for granted: Normal speech is not perfect. It is filled with hesitations, repetitions, prolongations, *ohs* and *uhs*, sighs—what I call "bobbles."

Most of us do pause when we speak. We do make mistakes. But we pay no attention to these *minor* imperfections and continue dialogue without concern for them. Stutterers, however, find it hard to accept that bobbles have a legitimate place in speech.

I advise these patients to listen more carefully to the way nonstutterers speak, to tune in to their pauses, hesitations, prolongations in the course of conversation. Furthermore, I require their listening to certain talk shows on radio and television, again to observe that even celebrity interviewees put bobbles into their speech. This is a first step in acquainting stutterers with the reality of verbal expression. Once they can hear these bobbles in what is considered "normal" conversation, they can begin the transition to a more sensible and practical voice image in themselves.

Some stutterers resist this alteration in speech attitude, and quite understandably, since their handicap has usually been with them for a long time. It customarily begins between the ages of three and seven. Adult stutterers thus face conversion to a new image of acceptable speech after a virtual lifetime of embracing an illusion about vocal expression.

One such patient, a young man in his twenties, refused to accept bobbles as a function of normal speech.

He consistently invoked the examples of television and radio announcers, as well as news broadcasters. Their voices might be flawed, he allowed, but their speech was fluid, constant, and perfect. I couldn't dissuade him from his point of view even when I proved to him that announcers and reporters *read* their material, and so are not proper models of conventional speech.

"Even 'the Fonz' doesn't talk with bobbles," he declared, "and *he's* not reading his lines. He does a whole show in front of an audience, without one mistake."

Like many young Americans, this twenty-two-year-old had grown up with the cast of the "Happy Days" situation comedy. So I arranged for us to attend a taping of one of their shows.

I sat next to my patient but said nothing as Henry Winkler and Ron Howard and the rest of their cast bobbled their way through a taping. One scene was reshot sixteen times until it was performed perfectly. The *ohs* and *uhs*, as well as their hesitations and repetitions would have been very acceptable in *real* conversation, mind you, but these minor unmistakable imperfections would not play on national television.

When the show ended, I sat in silence for a moment. Finally, I turned to my young friend. "So, what do you think?" I asked.

He laughed and slapped his knee. "You're not k-k-k-kidding me," he answered. "I know you asked them to put those bobbles in for m-m-m-m-me!"

In time, even this stalwart stutterer gave up his misguided notion of perfect speech, however, and made the change to healthy speech patterns—as well as healthy voice patterns, with his voice in the mask, complemented by proper tone focus.

He also learned to differentiate between hard and soft contact of the tongue while speaking. In hard contact, the tongue becomes still and presses against the teeth or the roof of the mouth. This happens because the stutterer learns to fear certain sounds and thus pre-forms them. But the tongue then interferes with speech, blocking not only sound, but the breathing process as well. Indeed, stutterers, like many in society, don't breathe at all while they talk when they are tense or pressured. Sometimes they hold their breath when they speak. Or they inhale, exhale immediately, and then proceed to talk without any breath support whatsoever. This habit is particularly common among stutterers and spastic dysphonics, but is not really unusual in the general public.

Once correct breathing has been implemented, the stutterer then works on achieving *soft* contact of the tongue when talking, allowing it to move freely and fluidly to pronounce and form sounds as they are required—not as they are anticipated. This is a gradual process during which the patient literally reeducates himself to think ahead in ideas and concepts, rather than in specific sounds. This allows the tongue to stay relaxed and to make soft contact within the mouth as thoughts are spontaneously articulated.

The intent here, as with all voice or speech deficiencies, is to help the individual achieve his natural right voice, as well as a positive speech *and* voice image. This new image is absolutely essential in the stutterer, for without it he cannot abandon his initial fear of imperfect speech.

Years ago, a lawyer from San Francisco came to me for help in overcoming a very serious stutter. Benjamin Moricone had had the condition since the age of six. He had hoped, actually, that the extra discipline and self-control required in the study of law would enable him to master his speech impediment. But his goal didn't materialize as he'd envisioned.

On graduation day, as each new attorney marched to

the podium and called out his name upon receiving a diploma, Benjamin grew more nervous. He wanted this day to proceed perfectly. Finally, his turn came.

He reached the stage, accepted his degree, and turned to the microphone to announce his name: "B-b-b-b- . . ." he began.

The ceremony came to a complete and embarrassing halt for two minutes as the anguished graduate tried to force out sounds that were not forthcoming.

Benjamin Moricone did not, needless to say, become a trial lawyer with an impressive vocal presence, as he had wished. But after many years in research, he heard about my methods of treatment and arranged an appointment. When I asked him what he wished to achieve in therapy, he said, "I want to talk perfectly." He was shocked when I explained that his quest for perfection had initiated his speech problem.

It took almost a year for Benjamin to fully abandon his old speech and voice habits, and assimilate new ones. But he did, at last, make the transition to healthy, successful voice use.

Soon thereafter, he and his wife went to Boston to visit Benjamin's mother. Upon hearing her son talk, Mrs. Moricone screamed, and then exclaimed: "You're not stuttering! Your speech is perfect!"

"No, mother," Benjamin replied, "it's not perfect. In fact, it's *im*perfect. But it works. After all these years, it works."

He had, indeed, overcome his fear and anxiety about communication.

FEELING STATES AND THE VOICE

Other types of fear, though, can initiate speech or voice disorders. Trauma, such as an accident, a sudden brush with death, an illness, or a loss, occasionally signals the onset of stuttering. It can also mark the beginning of a voice dysfunction, such as a condition called spastic dysphonia.

What happens in these instances is that once the trauma has passed, and even if it has been dealt with in traditional psychotherapy, the dysfunction remains.

In the case of stuttering—a speech disorder which often has voice misuse as a component—the treatment remains pretty much as described above. The speech image and the voice image are modified, and the mechanics of speech and voice usage are learned and implemented.

But as soon as one introduces the concept of feeling states as a causal ingredient of a speech or voice disorder, the whole issue of functional rehabilitation too often gets ignored or lost in the therapeutic process.

It is important to recognize that feeling states do, and should, reveal themselves in the voice. Expressions and intonations of anger, love, frustration, confusion, sadness, happiness are a critical part of vocal communication. But it is imperative that our emotions not *take control* of *how* we produce our voices.

Peggy Stewart, for example, was deeply affected and distressed by the loss of a close friend to leukemia. Her sadness was understandably reflected in her voice. But even as she adjusted to her loss and gradually resumed the regular activities of her life, her new voice habits—somber in tone, and projected from the lower throat—remained. Eventually, her voice misuse, now incorporated as an altered and habitual voice image, developed into constant laryngitis.

It is this combination of factors—voice misuse coupled with feeling states that may or may not still be present—that frustrates and confuses not only the victim but the medical establishment.

This is where direct voice rehabilitation enters as a necessary therapy, for it retrains the victim of voice suicide in the functional use of his voice—whatever the *contributory* causes of his voice dysfunction. Fortunately for Peggy, her vocal abuse was corrected, using my simple "technology," before it progressed further. Many others are not so lucky, particularly those who suffer from the most disabling of all disorders caused by voice misuse, the spastic dysphonics.

Before you can understand the attendant horrors of this condition, you should attempt to imagine how someone with spastic dysphonia sounds when he or she speaks. You may never have heard such a voice, or, if you have, you have most likely found it to be so alienating, so stunningly *alien*, that you made a hasty escape from it.

The spastic voice does not, in fact, sound as though it is of this world. It tends to be crackly, squeezed, and broken, with only minimal intelligibility. Usually, it has a groaning quality to it which distorts speech and obscures words or whole parts of sentences. It is, most of all, a tortured sound.

If you want to have a more precise concept of how this voice presents itself, you can produce a marginal fascimile of it by carrying out the following: Take a deep breath; now expel *all* air within you until your midsection and your chest feel concave; and start counting *out loud* to a hundred. By the time you reach thirty or forty, you probably will be taking on a "spastic" quality. Keep counting, without any breath intake. You'll soon get a sense of the spastic voice.

Now imagine that this is the *only* voice you can produce. And then try to imagine the way others look at you when you speak. Or when you try to respond to a question. Imagine performing your job with such a restrictive sound. Imagine making polite conversation at a cocktail party. Or reading a bedtime story to your children. Or answering the telephone. Or interviewing for a position with a new company. Lastly, imagine being told your condition is probably incurable. That's what happened to Chris Toberty.

By the time I first met Chris, she felt she was fighting for her sanity, as well as her voice. Not being able to speak in an intelligible manner was humiliating enough, but the psychological implications that had been drawn from her voice dysfunction dismayed her. She couldn't shake her recollection of one psychiatrist who had implied that her spastic dysphonia was self-induced, the result of guilt feelings over her repressed desire to have fellatio with her father.

Chris, by the way, is a veritable portrait of the middle- and upper middle-class New Jersey community in which she and her husband live. She has thick dark hair which falls loosely to her shoulders, a lovely frame for her classic features. Her shirtdresses and cardigans are traditional and unpretentious. Though the local country club has long been the center of an active social life, the Tobertys have always enjoyed frequent visits to New York City to take in shows, shopping, and elegant dinners.

Their lives were predictable, comfortable, and relatively calm over all the years they raised their family.

Then, in 1969, Bill Toberty became ill. Chris found herself carrying alone most of the burdens of raising three children, in addition to caring for her husband. It was a stressful time for her, but Chris marshalled her emotional resources and adeptly handled these changed circumstances. In time, Bill recovered his physical health. And the family eventually settled back into a happier routine.

In 1972, however, Chris's voice became persistently

hoarse. Over the next ten months, it gradually went spastic. Her family physician referred her to an ear-nose-throat specialist who started her on cortisone. The drug did not alleviate her problem, and Chris was soon under the care of both a psychiatrist and a speech therapist. When these specialists failed to resurrect her voice, Chris checked herself into a medical center on the East Coast.

There she worked with a speech therapist who advised her to keep her voice low, to add a breathy quality to her sound, and to employ upper-chest breathing. Meanwhile, the medical doctors at the institution uncovered no physical abnormalities and released her from care.

Returning home with a still-grotesque voice, Chris decided to try hypnosis as a cure. A series of sessions that emphasized relaxation techniques helped, and for the first time in two years Chris resumed partial function of her former voice. But the spastic dysphonia returned within eleven months.

Her family, by now, was having trouble coping with Chris's difficulties. Initially, husband and children alike feared she was suffering from throat cancer and were extremely supportive of her search for answers and solutions. But after all this, they unanimously concluded that her voice dysfunction might be psychosomatic in nature.

In 1978, desperate and increasingly isolated, Chris called a major midwestern medical institution. She was admitted soon after and in the next eight weeks was simultaneously under the care of medical personnel, a psychiatrist who focused on the management of stress, and a speech therapist who taught her tongue exercises. These various factions worked in concert to help Chris with her problem.

"The psychological counseling was good, actually,"

said Chris much later. "Looking back, that's all I remember as being helpful. I came to realize that I *had* been under stress a lot, and that I had never really known how to deal with pressures. I learned a great deal about myself. But I didn't learn how to get my voice back."

Back in New Jersey, Chris sought the help of another doctor. This one put her on drug therapy, starting with tranquilizers, and moving on to lithium in short order.

"It was a terrible time," she recalled. "I was terrified of the phone, of course, because I couldn't talk. And whenever I tried to talk, I couldn't get enough air to ward off that feeling of being strangled. I was always physically exhausted . . . and my vocabulary had suffered, too. Since speaking had become so hard, I'd begun resorting to monosyllabic words, to dropping adverbs and adjectives."

And she had ceased her attempts to communicate with her husband and children.

"It was so disturbing to [Bill] that I couldn't express myself as I always had, that I think he was relieved when I stopped trying to talk."

Finally, Chris once again checked herself into the medical center, where despite their collective efforts, the staff could offer no hope for a cure to her spastic dysphonia. She had three alternatives, she was told. She could accept her condition and learn to live with it. She could try another drug therapy. She could undergo an operation in which the laryngeal nerve would be cut. The surgery offered little hope for long-term relief, however. This procedure usually provided temporary, if any, results.

The surgery did not sound promising. And she was certainly unenthusiastic about resuming drug treatments. but she didn't want to passively accept her condition. No, she truly wished to return to her job with the

Historical Society; she longed to participate in club functions and other social affairs again; she yearned to spend time with her friends without fear of being mimicked. She couldn't do any of these things as long as she had spastic dysphonia.

Apparently as an afterthought, a staff member at the respected hospital mentioned my name. He said I had been working with spastic dysphonics, using a functional approach to recovery. My methods, it seems, were somewhat obscure but had been reported to be successful "in some cases."

This was a decision Chris had to make on her own. No one encouraged her or discouraged her to commit to any particular "last resort." Already, in the eleven years since the onset of her strangled voice, she had seen over thirty doctors and spent more than $50,000 on treatment and consultations. The financial strains as a result had been enormous. But she hated to succumb to her voice dysfunction. Her husband agreed, giving her the final push she needed to get on a plane to Los Angeles.

STOP STRANGLING YOURSELF

By the time patients such as Chris reach my office, they have usually been through so much turmoil, so many conflicting opinions, so many harrowing moments of voice dysfunction that it is often hard to convince them that their bad voice habits (innocently adopted) are quite literally strangling their own voices.

Constriction of the throat, misplaced pitch, and rigid voice images contribute to their disorder. So, too, do incorrect breathing techniques. Most spastic dysphonics breathe erratically when they attempt speech. Some expel all air before beginning to talk and thus have to forcefully push out a voice that has no fuel to keep it going. That's why you are able to mimic their sound when counting out loud with no breath support.

Chris related her long history to me in an effortful, spastic voice. Finally, I asked her to say "umm-hmmm," spontaneously and sincerely. She did.

"That's your right voice," I told her.

"What?" she said, returning immediately to the guttural spasticity.

Again I asked her to repeat "umm-hmmm," lips closed, with a rising inflection. Again, she did, in a clear and natural sound.

And so I began with Chris, as I began with you, to explain the elements of correct voice production—of optimal pitch, tone focus, quality, rate, volume, breath support. I described how the voice mechanism can be misused and abused to the point where it becomes dysfunctional. That it must then be retrained in order to restore proper functioning. I also told her that my professional experience had indicated that voice misuse, in combination with physical or psychological trauma—with trauma as the *catalyst*—caused spastic dysphonia in most occurrences.

Haunted by the conclusion of the psychiatrist who attributed her disorder to the repression of a desire to have fellatio with her father, Chris asked if I had ever before heard such a theory. I had heard countless theories, I told her. But what did it mean at this juncture? Did she think it was true? No. Did she believe she had purposely, albeit subconsciously, sabotaged her own ability to speak? No. Then what did it matter what one man thought? Our purpose was to restore the functional use of her voice. Wasn't that what she came to achieve? Yes. Then I would help her regain control of the voice that had for so long controlled her.

We talked about voice images—negative and positive. Together we performed the exercises—the counting, the instant voice press, the reading aloud. We practiced with energy words. And by our second session, Chris was able to produce a voice without my direct guidance. This was still a strained voice, mind you, but it represented a vast improvement. After three weeks in voice retraining, Chris worked up the courage to use the telephone. Her functional voice use was still far from being completely restored—and by that I mean healthy, dynamic, effortless, natural—but Chris now had hope, which she hadn't had for a long time.

"The easier it gets, the more confidence I have," she declared. "And the more confidence I have, the easier it gets." She was on her way, though Chris still requires a great deal of direct guidance before she can successfully complete a carry-over of her natural voice from the office situation into her regular activities.

Spastic dysphonia is not "cured" overnight. Each patient requires his own pace in the retraining process. It takes time, patience, and discipline to undo the harmful habits that have continuously been used for years. The fundamentals of correct voice production apply to the care and treatment of spastic dysphonia every bit as much as they apply to the treatment of other forms of voice abuse. Here, as always, we stress the achievement of correct, or optimal, pitch, as well as tone focus. But perhaps more than in any other voice disorder except stuttering, we work on correct breathing techniques.

The strangling sensation Chris experienced was just that: The combined constriction of the throat area and the total lack of breath support served to strangle the voice box. No wonder sound has such difficulty in emerging. Still, many patients resist applying the basics of voice health, but only because they perceive them to be too simple a remedy after prolonged and disabling voice dysfunction.

Barry Farnsworth, for one, did just that.

Ironically, Barry was a professor of *communications* at a large Southwestern university when his spastic dysphonia began. Unlike Chris Toberty, he never came under the care of a psychiatrist during his five years of voice spasticity, but he also tried just about anything he could think of to resolve his problem.

After numerous medical consultations which provided no keen insights into his difficulties, Barry attempted many other remedies, fourteen in all, to exorcise the demon sound that had overtaken him. Among them were acupuncture, yoga, allergy testing and treatment, meditation, exercise, biofeedback. The results were nil. He sought treatment at a well-known California medical center, again with no results. And he worked with a speech therapist who suggested he employ a falsetto voice. Again, he met with failure, in part because this high sound was very hard for him to produce, and in part because he found it almost as alienating a sound as the spasticity.

Barry also consulted a surgeon who recommended cutting his laryngeal nerve. The doctor apparently claimed that spastic dysphonia was caused by a virus. But Barry denied having had a virus and, in addition, had already been tested for neurological involvement which might have developed secondary to a virus, and these tests had proved negative. So he rejected this course, too.

Barry is an academic, a cerebral man, so perhaps that is why he described *my* methods of voice rehabilitation as "too simple, too simplistic." Despite his skepticism, however, he returned for treatment week after week over the next year. While he could produce a functional voice with my direct supervision, he could not seem to do so on his own. Then, at last, and undoubtedly to his own surprise, he apparently experienced a vocal catharsis. He progressed slowly but surely after that moment.

Months later, he attended a lecture I had been asked to give at Cedars-Sinai Hospital in Los Angeles. By now the bearer of a well-functioning, healthy voice, Barry told the gathering of ear-nose-throat specialists in the room that my rehabilitative techniques for the treatment of spastic dysphonia were "simple . . . and effective."

Barry, initially a skeptic, became a believer. He learned not to let the myriad stresses in his life manifest themselves in voice misuse and abuse. And he achieved, without surgery, a complete recovery of a normal voice through functional retraining in the use of his voice.

Donald Schaefer, an oil man from Texas, adds yet another variable to the list of incredible experiences common to victims of spastic dysphonia.

His initial vocal strain manifested itself, curiously, in a rapid blinking of his eyes which he could not seem to control. Medical consultations and testing revealed neither cause nor explanations for his problem. Nor were solutions offered to reduce the blinking.

It took a while, almost a year, before Donald himself realized what none of his doctors noticed. His voice was quickly going out; and further, his rapid eye blinking seemed directly related to the voice difficulty. The harder he pushed his voice to work, the more he blinked. This "tic" had developed, it seemed, as a result of vocal difficulties that had formerly gone undetected. Psychotherapy was recommended and pursued. Still, his condition worsened. Finally, Donald opted to seek help at the best-known medical facility he could think of for his now totally spastic voice.

There, he underwent "voice testing" as well as ophthalmic examination. "They concentrated on the blinking," said Donald, "but offered no ideas as to cause or recovery, either of the 'tic' or the spastic dysphonia. In fact, it wasn't long before they told me my condition was hopeless."

One of the doctors at the hospital described the experimental surgery in which the laryngeal nerve is cut. No promises were made, no encouragement offered, but Donald was growing desperate over his voice dysfunction. He elected to try the surgery. He soon regretted his decision.

After the surgery, he found, his voice was worse than it had been prior to the procedure. "Some days it was high, some days it was low and spastic. Some days it didn't work at all. My voice was in a constant state of flux, contorted and distorted. As crazy as this may sound, I wished it would just return to spasticity again."

His wish was fulfilled. Donald's voice reverted to its former state about six months after the surgery. And now he was left to start all over again in search of a solution. Eventually, he was referred to my office for voice retraining. The bit of improvement he experienced at his first session impressed him, though he reserved final judgment pending long-term results.

"Spastic dysphonia is a humiliating condition," he said at the time. "It blocks you from the process of communicating. And it also makes you cynical when you discover you can't get help from medical specialists. They either don't know or aren't interested. You end up feeling distrustful of the whole medical establishment."

After several months of voice therapy, he agreed he had made considerable progress in overcoming his voice dysfunction. "My voice works well about half the time now. That's a lot better than none of the time." His pitch was properly placed when he spoke. His sound had tone focus. He was providing good midsection breath support.

A casual observer who was visiting the office remarked to Donald that she would never have known he had a voice problem had he not mentioned it. "Your voice sounds at least as good, certainly as 'normal,' as any voice I've heard today. . . ."

Donald furrowed his brow in contemplation of this assessment. "Oh, no," he said at last, speaking in a clear, efficient voice. "I still have spastic dysphonia, can't you tell?"

This declaration is telling and elucidating in that it aptly depicts the importance of voice image in the individual. Donald was clearly *mastering the mechanics of correct voice usage,* as indicated by the fact that he could effectively employ them much of the time in my office. When he did, his sound was neither spastic nor troubled. But he had not yet made the transition to a new sound concept of himself. He had not yet experienced vocal catharsis. Until this occurred, his self-identity would to a great degree be defined by his old, habitual voice image, that of the spastic dysphonic.

It should also be noted that Donald had been told his condition was "hopeless." Yet only several months later he was fairly consistently producing a strong, *functional* voice in my office that had few, if any, telltale signs of spasticity.

Again and again, we see the benefits derived from the use of the basic elements of voice production, the fundamentals of voice success and health: the achievement of correct pitch; tone focus; rate; volume; quality; breath support. These mechanics apply to you, whether your voice is "merely" unattractive or moderately deficient or severely dysfunctional.

That is why I often refer to this simple method of voice management as a "sound revolution." Efficient, magical voice communication has never been more vital and necessary than it is today. If you want to improve the sound you make every time you open your mouth to speak, all you need do is join the revolution.

EQUALITY FOR ALL

You have probably discerned that there is no socio-economic bias in the occurrence of voice disorders. Without voice training—and that means without proper instruction in the correct use of the voice—everyone is susceptible to voice dysfunction. My patient roster proves this point.

Even the most severe and disabling of voice dysfunctions, spastic dysphonia, afflicts individuals from all walks of life. I have treated teachers, homemakers, doctors, lawyers, scientists, telephone operators, artists, business executives, movie producers, secretaries, and others for this disturbing condition. And there is one rule above all others that holds fast: Misuse of the vocal mechanism is always present, irrespective of any other contributory factors. Furthermore, retraining in the functional use of the voice is always indicated and is essential.

Each victim of voice suicide—whatever the form of his or her voice dysfunction—requires a different length of time in the retraining process. Some individuals progress rapidly, others slowly. Many have difficulty maintaining optimal pitch, while others have trouble incorporating correct breathing techniques. Not a few resist, despite all good intentions, adopting a new voice image. Individual or special problems, however, should not preclude success. So be patient with yourself in the gradual attainment of these elements of correct voice use.

There is as much equality in voice rehabilitation as there is in the incidence of voice suicide. Ultimately, the decisive factor will fall to you: You must want to overcome your voice handicap. You must be persistent in the application of the elements of voice health that have been previously outlined (and which will soon be reviewed). You must want to be better than you are.

ON BEING GOOD TO YOURSELF

Whether your voice is mildly deficient or seriously dysfunctional, whether it "merely" sells you short or incapacitates you, if you wish to improve the quality of your own sound, you must confront one inescapable fact: Change will not occur unless *you* take responsibility for your own voice and make it occur.

There is no magic pill to locate and sustain optimal pitch. There is no medical procedure which initiates correct breathing techniques. No surgery that removes a negative voice image and implants a positive voice image. There is, however, a *method,* as outlined in this book, for achieving voice magic as well as voice health.

This method of direct voice retraining requires a certain amount of concentration, practice, and self-discipline, that's true. But the rewards of mastering these fundamentals of voice use can extend to many areas of your life.

Many of my patients say that it's all part of being good to themselves. That they want not only to overcome their vocal handicaps but to become more healthy, more dynamic, more compelling in presenting themselves to the world.

That's what Jana Hoffman, a twenty-one-year-old USC drama student, wanted when she sought my help. Her recurrent laryngitis—the result of voice misuse— was responsible for the growth of nodes on her larynx. Direct voice rehabilitation caused the nodes to recede and disappear. And Jana's new, right voice helped land her a part in a stage production. It was a role that previously had been denied her because her voice wouldn't carry.

Economist Sidney Fields found that the soreness in his throat and the ache in his chest finally vanished after he acquired healthy voice techniques. And he was glad to be rid of his froggy-bottom voice. "People listen to what I say, now that I have a good voice."

John Dahlman decided that voice retraining was better than a second surgery to treat a precancerous condition of his larynx. The papilomatosis resolved, in time, and John was able to resume his career in the sales of healthcare equipment.

And Judith Wilson, a tall, exotic beauty who just happens to be a mechanical systems engineer on guided missiles, actually *enjoyed* learning this new and simple voice "technology." Her voice had gone out two years after she had been appointed spokesperson to the Air Force and Army on the development and deployment of classified programs. "I'm sorry I got this condition," she reported, "but at least I'm finally learning to use my voice correctly."

These patients, along with many others, exemplify the gains to be made by acquiring dynamic and healthy voice production. By being good to themselves, they were good to their voices. It's all part of a dynamic often referred to as "self-realization," which is the fulfillment of one's own greatest potential. Yes, achieving the use of your right natural voice *is* an integral element of meeting *your* greatest potential.

THE CASES THAT NEED SPECIALIZED HELP

I do not mean to suggest that *all* individuals will be able to achieve this potential on their own, without direct guidance. I have attempted to describe the elements of correct voice production in terms that anyone and everyone can understand and employ. But some victims of voice suicide, those with the most serious forms of voice dysfunction, may need more personalized help than is possible in printed form.

If you are a victim of spastic dysphonia or a paralyzed vocal fold, in particular, you will need to work with a voice therapist in applying the principles outlined in this book. Any sort of advanced pathology is harder to overcome only because it has been allowed to progress to an extreme and severe state.

There's no reason, however, that you shouldn't try to implement these steps on an independent basis. You would be smart, of course, to have a partner or associate join you in the retraining process. The added emotional support alone might be enough to get you past the barriers that present themselves.

Whatever your initial results, don't despair. Don't lose hope. Go back and try again, starting with the attainment of optimal pitch and balanced tone focus. Make adjustments as necessary until your "umm-hmmm" produces that slight tingling or vibration about the nose and mouth that will signify balanced oral-nasal resonance. Slow your rate of speech, if necessary, so that you can concentrate on the mechanics. And by all means, get to work on the breathing techniques. The exercises are easy to perform. Repeat them over and over. Midsection breath support will eventually become routine to you. Now practice reading aloud into a tape recorder, employing your newly acquired correct pitch and breathing procedures.

Do ponder and discuss the effect of voice images in both the use of your old, habitual voice and your new, right voice. You might be surprised to find yourself clinging to images that are negative rather than positive.

If so, ask yourself why and to what end you refuse to abandon a sound concept that has probably inflicted harm. And search for better voice models.

Tune in the "Tonight Show" and listen to the way Johnny Carson uses his voice, placing it in the mask and enhancing it with correct tone focus. Watch a movie starring Anthony Quinn. Pay attention to his sound. It's healthy and dynamic. So is Burt Reynolds's. And Cary Grant's.

I have often, throughout this book and in my day-to-day encounters, described my techniques for voice success as "simple." They are, in that they are direct and clear-cut and effective. In other words, they produce *results*. Keep in mind that every individual masters these techniques at his or her own pace.

And if you are concerned about the psychological or physical trauma that may have helped precipitate your voice dysfunction, be aware that you may not be able to trace it back to a specific instance. Sometimes a jolt to either your body or emotions has occurred long ago and initiated voice misuse which may have slowly progressed into a serious disorder.

And keep in mind that trauma doesn't have to be a thunderbolt. Psychological factors don't need to be immediate or urgent. Sometimes they *do* build up and turn to stress, and stress can tense the body, inwardly and outwardly. Stress can tense the vocal equipment and set voice misuse in motion.

Stress is part of life, of course. So the key here is to learn good voice habits and to use them even during the inevitable anxious periods of your life. Your new voice consciousness should, in fact, cause you to be aware of lapses in healthy voice use and enable you to make quick and appropriate corrections.

But again, those of you with serious dysfunction may

indeed require special assistance to effect your new voice consciousness. If you are having trouble mastering these fundamentals and restoring vitality to your voice, seek the help of a voice therapist. Emphasize that you want retraining in the functional use of your voice through the achievement of optimal pitch, balanced tone focus, and midsection breathing.

And still, if you don't find the specific help you are looking for in your immediate area, do not give up. Both the medical establishment and the field of voice rehabilitation are now awakening to the value of this direct retraining process. They are themselves only beginning to understand that voice misuse and abuse are primary causes of voice dysfunction, and that correct voice techniques are required to attain and sustain voice health. But the word is spreading quickly. I hope there will soon be a practitioner of direct voice rehabilitation in most communities in the nation.

Meanwhile, keep practicing on your own. Do not despair, even if your voice dysfunction has been with you for a long time or if it has isolated you from the people and activities you most love. The results I have achieved in my practice demonstrate an excellent prognosis for almost all voice ills through the application of direct voice rehabilitation.

7

Don't Fight Success

The voice is a wonderful instrument. It permits us to express our every idea, wish, emotion, anxiety, fear, frustration—instantaneously and to whomever or whatever we care to address. Some people even find that it's helpful to close themselves off in a room and conduct verbal discussions with themselves. This mere act—of articulating the thought processes, of presenting the pros and cons of an issue or crisis—often allows mental clarity to be most quickly achieved. But this extraordinary instrument that permits speech sometimes goes bad, becomes inoperative, leaving its unwitting victims stranded in a world that is almost impossible to navigate without a functional voice.

Whatever your manner or mode of voice distress, there is almost always hope, there is help to be had. If you suffer, simply, from functional wrong voice, you can improve your sound. If you are one of many who has been immobilized by a serious voice dysfunction, you can most likely revive your voice, and attain a clear, dynamic sound that will serve you well.

As you have seen, I have treated almost every imaginable type of voice problem. My methods of voice man-

158

agement have produced results in patients with hoarseness, laryngitis, nasality, falsetto voice, stuttering, spastic dysphonia. In patients young and old. In patients from all walks of life, from all socioeconomic levels. Even in patients who suffer from a paralyzed vocal cord.

This condition results from many causes. Sometimes it is idiopathic in nature, with no clear genesis. Or it can initiate with a virus that attacks the larynx. Often it occurs because of a surgical "accident," in which the nerve is inadvertently cut in the course of a throat or chest operation. In any of these events, the voice becomes erratic and unpredictable. Sometimes it is high-pitched, sometimes it is low-pitched. Sometimes it is breathy. These were the characteristics of Donald Schaefer's voice after he underwent this procedure *on purpose*, in the hope that his spastic voice would regain function. As I noted, this new form of dysfunction was more troublesome for Donald than his spastic dysphonia.

Richard Jones ended up with this condition after undergoing a thyroidectomy during which his laryngeal nerve was accidentally severed. But this was one of the known risks and Richard was told quite tersely that there was no form of treatment to correct his "errant" sound that traveled through many voice zones in the course of every conversation. This wandering voice in search of a home base eventually found its way to my office, however. Through direct voice retraining, Richard gained control of his voice at last, and despite having been told he would have to live forever with this condition. Today, he has a well-functioning, clear, efficient sound. And thank goodness. It makes his job as an air traffic controller a lot easier!

LAUGH EVEN THOUGH YOUR VOICE IS "BROKEN"

If you think I'm being glib, well, perhaps you are right. But laughter is a good way to release tension. Have you ever noticed that some people under dire pressures or in profound grief *need* to laugh? The old "Mary Tyler Moore Show" built an entire episode on this premise, that bottled-up emotions often find laughter as their only escape. In her case, Mary broke into uncontrollable laughter during the funeral of Chuckles the Clown. It was funny *and* very human in its treatment. I've seen this sort of thing happen a number of times in real life, too. But of course, this is a kind of hysterical response to stress or mourning, and thus tends to produce a "hysterical" laugh.

Spontaneous, natural laughter—*sincere* laughter—is actually good in many ways. It still serves as a kind of release, apparently, though its real function and purpose is not understood. Norman Cousins, in a book called *Anatomy of an Illness,* described how he used laughter as a tool for overcoming a life-threatening disease. But laughter can even be used as a tool in the voice retraining process.

Many patients discover that their own laugh—when it is totally spontaneous and *real*—is a perfect reflection of their optimal pitch. When it is natural, laughter is usually produced at the right physiological level; in other words, as nature intended and without constraints.

Another amusing means of achieving optimal pitch is to perform a headstand. Yes, that's right, the inverted position of the headstand breaks the body armor and often produces a functional, well-placed voice in people who are otherwise incapable of making voice sounds.

Maybe that's why Judith Wilson, the beautiful mechanical systems engineer on guided missiles, enjoyed her voice rehabilitation so much. She practiced her voice exercises every morning while standing on her head.

REASONS FOR FAILURE IN VOICE RETRAINING

I hope by now you have the motivation to master the elements of correct voice production using the techniques I have described. This method does take practice and time, but the rewards can be great. Some few people, however, will not be able to retrain their functional voice use without the help of a competent voice therapist. This is reasonable and understandable in individuals who, as we have already noted, suffer from serious voice dysfunction and pathology. The barriers are greater for them as well as for those who do not follow written directions well. And I highly recommend they seek the extra assistance and guidance of a professional. I urge anyone with *persistent* hoarseness, throat pain, or inability to produce speech sounds to consult a medical doctor.

Some others, however will not follow through on voice retraining, despite their ability to do so on their own. It goes without saying, of course, that among the reasons for abandoning this path to voice health, success, magic, is laziness. Certain individuals will continue in their search for a magic pill or a costly operation to heal their voice ills. They won't want to assume responsibility.

A few readers, though, will still resist this easy and direct retraining process because they have never before heard of voice health or voice management. The lack of education relevant to the use of the speaking voice is widespread, more the rule than the exception, throughout our society. I advise you now that as the veritable epidemic of voice misuse and abuse in this country escalates, voice health and voice use will finally be more widely discussed. Voice techniques will be taught. You can choose to improve your own sound in the interim, or you can take your chances and wait. Wait for what, you ask?

No, I'm not threatening you with dreaded consequences. Not every voice will go out or become spastic because of voice abuse. Not every voice will alienate others as a result of nasal tones or throaty huskiness. Indeed, not every individual even cares if his or her voice is effective or compelling. But I am a bit of a zealot, and I do believe that we all want to be liked, to be accepted, to be approved of. And I know from experience that the voice is perceived for its negative or positive qualities, that it does influence the way we are received by the society about us. I also suspect that this issue of voice will be increasingly factored into the professional and personal guides to achieving success. So my question to you is, *why risk waiting* until the competition is so stiff it gets the better of you?

Success is not truly desired by everyone, though. I have observed this in more than a few instances in the course of treating patients. Some victims of voice suicide use a vocal handicap as a tool for attention. Pity, however demeaning, is sometimes considered better than no attention at all. In fact, as we have discussed, an effective and commanding voice generates *positive* attention. And that is by far the best form of personal notice one can find.

But a dysfunctional voice can and is occasionally used to sustain a dependency. These are the hardest cases to treat, naturally, because the patient has some emotional or financial interest in perpetuating the disorder. Here, the individual *cannot* (subconsciously), or *will not* (consciously), let go of an old voice image and adopt a new image. This is often a sign of fear—fear of returning to work, fear of social intercourse, fear of putting oneself on the line in life. It is truly tragic to see someone hide behind a voice disability. But these cases are rare indeed. The key to recovery in such individuals *seems* often to be subtle but lovingly supportive coercion by family or employers. Aggressive force might well drive such victims to retreat further into their isolation.

PLATEAUS

Some individuals make initial progress in the retraining of their voices, then reach a plateau. In the case of Donald Schaefer, who suffered from spastic dysphonia, we saw that he was in the process of mastering all the mechanics of correct voice usage, but had not tackled the matter of adopting a new voice image.

Perhaps you, for example, have achieved optimal pitch, balanced tone focus, good quality and rate, and appropriate volume. You may love your new voice image. But you may have difficulty using proper breathing techniques when you speak.

Plateaus are as common among voice patients as they are among any sector of society implementing any new training. Tennis players reach plateaus in their games. Runners often reach plateaus in terms of distance when beginning the sport. Most people reach plateaus in their careers.

Some, at this point, give up. In the professions, it is not unusual to see people reach a plateau and then level out, accepting this state of affairs as a sign that they have achieved their peak. Performance then may even slide downward. The same trend can be observed in athletic endeavors. Haven't you known someone who took up running for its cardiovascular benefits, and who after a couple of weeks noticed he couldn't surpass his two-mile limit? And who then surrendered to defeat because he wasn't the marathoner he'd dreamed of becoming?

In fact, with continued perseverance and practice, this runner would certainly have achieved greater distances. Maybe he wouldn't have become James Fixx, but he would have been better and more successful than he permitted himself to be.

And haven't we all remarked at one time or another that a friend or acquaintance achieved greatness as a result of will, persistence, and the refusal to abandon his goals?

You can apply these same traits to the voice retraining process. If you reach a plateau and give up, you will nevertheless be more accomplished in the voice game than you were. But if you decide to practice some more, to concentrate a little bit harder on providing midsection breath support to your voice, well, you, too, can come closer to your goal. You might even achieve that status of voice magic!

REGRESSION

Regression or lapses occur during the retraining period. By anticipating them, you can avoid becoming discouraged. You may find, for instance, that an intimate telephone conversation or a frenzied circumstance causes you to lose control of your pitch level and tone focus. A cold or a respiratory ailment, or an emotional trauma, could push your voice to an improper pitch. But you know *how* to locate and determine your own pitch and tone focus now, so all you need to do if such a lapse occurs is go back to the "umm-hmmm" and practice it a few times. Perform an instant voice press. Read aloud. In other words, reacquaint yourself with your right voice. And remember, in time and with practice, your natural voice will be comfortable and easy to produce in any situation. It will be so familiar and routine that you probably won't lose it at all.

But don't ignore regression. Accept it as a natural, normal part of the newness of your right voice use. And then use the simple elements you have learned to restore correct functioning.

VOICE HYGIENE

You should treat your voice with respect. It is a vital ingredient in your self-presentation. If you care for it, if you use it properly, it should not tire or fail or go hoarse or develop pathology. You are the keeper of your body. You are thus the protector of the physiologic mechanism that allows for speech. As I said earlier, your voice can help you find love, acceptance, approval, respect. It can also cause you to be rejected, fired, disliked, or ignored. You use your voice to tell the world *who* you are and *what* you think. Its effectiveness depends to a great degree on HOW you use it.

Here are some tips to help you care for this crucial tool of self expression:

—Attempt to maintain an optimal or natural pitch level with moderate volume at all times, even when experiencing a cold or upper respiratory infection. Do not purposely try to "pamper" your voice during times of stress of illness by letting it drop to the lower throat. You will do it more harm than good, and might even fall back into your old, habitual voice.

—Generally curtail smoking and drinking, if excessive.

—Avoid competing with very loud noises. If you are at an airport and a jet is taking off, wait until the airliner has passed before continuing conversation. If you are in a loud construction area, talk only when necessary. When at a cocktail party or other large gathering, talk *into* noise, rather than attempting to talk above it or below it.

—Attempt to refrain from excessive yelling or screaming at ballgames or during other recreational activities. Shouting at times is normal and acceptable, but constant bellowing isn't good. Besides annoying your neighbors, it might injure your voice box.

—Try to minimize repeated violent physical disturbances, such as coughing and clearing of the throat.

—Be alert to signs of distress. If your voice feels tired and in need of a rest, you are misusing it.

—Continue maximum use of your right, natural voice, using moderate volume and correct breathing techniques.

FOR THE YOUNG AND THE OLD, TOO

The precepts of healthy voice production as described in this book apply to children and also to senior citizens. Children, who invariably receive no voice training, tend to yell and scream. When their voices go hoarse from this misuse and abuse, they just love to continue yelling and screaming even if they can no longer produce sound. Use good judgment if your children are prone to such excesses. Educate them gradually in the correct use of their voices. Without such guidance, children are susceptible to nodes and other growths on the vocal cords which might require surgical excision. They are particularly vulnerable to developing negative voice habits, unless otherwise instructed. Give them an advantage that you didn't have: a positive voice model and an education in the use of their voices.

Be sensitive to the senior citizens in your family or work place. As people advance into old age, many, quite simply, grow tired. Their own lack of voice training often results in a voice that falls to the lower throat. Or a primary disease or sickness might cause an older individual to employ a somber, defeated tone, projected from the lower one-third, which in turn could initiate another physical disorder, this one the result of voice abuse.

If you notice such a tendency in your mother or father, or grandparents, or some other senior citizen who is close to you, gently encourage the individual to place his pitch and tone focus in the mask. Say that you miss the lighthearted voice of old, or that you yourself need help in the retraining of your own voice.

In other words, share the magic!

LETTING GO OF THE OLD, WELCOMING THE NEW

The tools of successful voice production are now yours. You can have a voice that draws others into its spell, a resonant sound that virtually hypnotizes your listeners into accepting your point of view. The implementation of these tools is not too great a task, especially when you consider the benefits to be gained. You will have to practice until the elements of correct voice use are so routine, so familiar that they occur spontaneously. You can keep your motivation strong by reminding yourself every morning that the manner in which you vocally express yourself is the key to your identity.

The world will thus judge you as you judge others: by the voice image you project every time you speak. Make your voice image compelling, dynamic, healthy—by learning to use your right, natural voice.

That's what a young man named Moshe did when he came all the way from Israel in search of a solution to his spastic dysphonia. Though no one had yet given a name to his voice disorder, he was convinced he would eventually find an explanation, as well as a cure, if only he kept up his pursuit. He had been to London and Boston and New York before reaching my office. An ear-nose-throat doctor in Manhattan had actually instructed him to chew on a golf ball to relax the apparent constriction about his throat.

Eager to try anything by that time, Moshe did try the golf ball treatment, only to break a couple of teeth. He had caps made at a local dentist's office during the course of his therapy in my office. It wasn't long before he once again had a beautiful smile—which handsomely complemented his now healthy, now resonant voice.

And Crystal Lauck, too, mastered the elements of correct voice production, despite suffering from spastic dysphonia for four years. She appeared in my office one day after rejecting the advice of a Beverly Hills specialist who advised her to take Valium and play lots of tennis if she hoped to recover from her voice dysfunction. She didn't need tranquilizers, she declared, and she happened not to like tennis. After six months of functional retraining of her voice, she achieved complete resolution of her vocal difficulties.

Moshe and Crystal, like you, sought and eventually found practical solutions to voice deficiencies. They, like you, determined to slowly let go of the old sound concept and gradually permit themselves to embrace the new. They, like you, came to understand the voice as an integral element in all that defines each individual as a special, unique person.

Which is exactly what you are!

Your own, natural, right voice is the sound that can best present you to a judgmental world. This special voice that is yours is waiting to be discovered—and loved.

8

Charting Your Course

We started this book by talking about people who have that intangible power that commands attention and generates success. We showed that this special gift to persuade and convince and attract is in the voice—in the mask, to be precise.

Franklin Delano Roosevelt had the power. So did Sir Winston Churchill. Jack Benny had a great voice. As does Bob Hope. And Cary Grant. And Audrey Hepburn. And Johnny Carson. And Orson Welles. And Anne Bancroft. And Burt Reynolds. The late Dr. Martin Luther King, Jr. was a master in the use of voice techniques. Each of these individuals presents a unique sound, but a sound nonetheless defined by excellent voice production.

But as you have seen, healthy and dynamic voice skills need not continue to be a special talent limited to a precious few. Now, at last, the elements of voice use are available to any and all who wish to benefit from them. They are simple, and direct, and require only discipline and concentration to achieve. With practice and time, they become second nature, with the result that a wonderful, engaging sound is consistently projected. This natural, right voice exists in each of us and

170

is just waiting to be discovered and used to best advantage. It's no wonder, then, that many people have joined this "sound revolution," as I like to call it.

Among the celebrities who have been instructed in my method of voice management are Cheryl Ladd, Norton Simon, Stevie Nicks, and Joan Rivers. Also, John Saxon, Jerome Hines, Lucille Ball, Dennis Weaver. And Diahann Carroll, Richard Crenna, Kirk Douglas, Marilyn Hassett, Phil Silvers, Richard Basehart, O. J. Simpson, and the late Henry Fonda who experienced a strangled voice.

Each of these individuals recognized the importance of a well-functioning and engaging voice; each set out to acquire the tools to achieve a sound that would enhance both the professional and personal sides of life. Each came to understand that the voice has a vital impact on all human relationships.

But my patient roster is hardly dominated by the names of the famous. It is populated by people from all walks and all stations of society.

The senior vice-president of Metro-Goldwyn-Mayer Studio, Peter Bart, had voice retraining. So did the president of Twentieth Century–Fox, Joe Wizan. And film producer Michael Gruskoff; and director John Frankenheimer. And countless others, including lawyers, teachers, business leaders, telephone operators, insurance salespersons, secretaries, homemakers, politicians, commodities traders, writers.

I treated an eminent writer not long ago, one who suffered from dysphasia after having experienced a stroke. Dysphasia is a loss or deficiency in the ability to use language after an injury to the brain. This writer who had long made a living with his masterful use of language couldn't remember how to say "table." He knew what he wanted to say, he knew what the object was, but he just couldn't find that right word.

I instructed him to keep talking, however frustrating it was to be constantly blocked from simple communication, communication that had formerly come so readily. He learned to talk "around" objects and ideas until, at last, self-expression became spontaneous and fluid once again. Family and friends patiently offered support and encouragement without stepping on his lines or interrupting him. During this reeducation period, the writer had to be retrained in the use of his speaking voice also, which was now deficient.

Like you, and all my patients, he was guided through the basics of voice use: pitch; tone focus; quality; volume; rate; breath support. This was a slow, arduous process. But he was determined, he was disciplined, and his will won out.

At the end of a year, this patient had regained full mastery of his former language skills—and had acquired a rich, healthy, dynamic voice. If he could do it, so, too, can you.

HERE'S TO THE FUTURE

I do see signs that the future will bring greater awareness of healthy voice usage. Despite encountering greater numbers of voice suicides in my private practice, I am at least comforted to know that appropriate help is now being sought by many for whom help was not formerly available.

More patients are being referred by medical doctors who have awakened not only to the dangers of voice misuse and abuse, but to the benefits of voice retraining. Indeed, these same physicians are often coming in for help with their own voices, and taking their newly acquired information on the subject back to their patients.

Medical institutions are finally becoming alert to the

value of functional voice retraining and healthy voice techniques. Not only are they, too, referring patients, but they are beginning to employ some of my methods of voice management. In time, I hope medical schools will catch on also, and make this a required subject for doctors in training.

In fact, many organizations are already taking the initiative by educating their own employees, their members, or their students in the subject of voice success and health. They have suddenly, of late, grasped the significance of these techniques and endeavored to use them to their own best advantage. Thus, I am often asked to address professional groups, management seminars, communications classes, and special societies.

In the meantime, many former patients who have already been down the disastrous path toward voice suicide and come back, through the acquisition of healthy voice habits, are sharing the tools of their own voice magic with friends, relatives, colleagues. Once you know what they are, the symptoms of voice misuse are easy to identify. And once negative voice traits are identified, they can be readily overcome. A little knowledge is all that's needed.

And I'm starting to notice some healthy voice models —at last!—on television news programs. Tom Brokaw and Peter Jennings and Bryant Gumble all have well-used voices. Dan Rather has an excellent voice. And so, too, will you.

YOU CAN DO IT!

Indeed, you have already come a long way in a short time. You have identified your own negative voice habits, and are learning to employ positive voice habits. You found your correct pitch through the "umm-hmmm" method and achieved proper tone focus at the same time. I call this a "two-for-oner." And as a result, you have achieved a better quality of voice.

Gradually, you will incorporate correct breathing techniques into your voice use, and find a comfortable but effective rate of speech. You will use moderate volume most of the time, and if you find you must shout on occasion, you'll at least shout correctly—with your voice placed in the mask and buttressed with breath support.

And with some practice and self-awareness, you will soon have adopted a new sound concept of yourself, which will reflect a positive and healthy voice image.

You now have all the tools you need to achieve your right voice. So go after the magic—that intangible power inherent in *your* natural voice.

The brief guide below will enable you to quickly review the exercises and rules of dynamic voice production. Refer to this summary as often as necessary during the re-training period.

REVIEWING THE STEPS

A good voice is projected from the mask. The mask includes the bridge and sides of the nose down to and around the lips. Speaking through the mask will open your sound, make your voice flexible, and fill it with expression and warmth. It will give carrying power and range, as well as facial (oral-nasal) resonance, which gives correct tone focus.

The first step in creating this voice of success is in finding your optimal pitch and a balanced tone focus.

Answer each of the statements below with a spontaneous and sincere "umm-hmmm." Use a rising inflection, with the lips closed:

—Winston Churchill was a noted orator and wartime leader.

—Franklin Delano Roosevelt is remembered as a president who possessed magnetism and great persuasive powers.

—I, too, would like to be skillful in the art of communication.

—My voice may be selling me short because I've never been educated to use it in an effective and healthy manner.

—For the first time, I am aware that the voice I've always used may not be the voice nature intended me to have.

—Since I would like to be the best person I can possibly be, I would be well-advised to learn the easy and straightforward techniques of correct voice production.

—By disciplining myself to use my natural, right voice in everyday conversation, I can use the inherent gift of speech to my best advantage.

Let's ease slowly and gradually toward producing the same pitch level in conversation. Be aware of the slight vibration that should be occurring about the nose and mouth.

Say "umm-hmmm-one." Now "umm-hmmm-two." "Umm-hmmm-three."

Is the pitch of the number at the same level as the "umm-hmmm"? Listen carefully to your own voice as you continue counting, preceding each number with a natural and sincere "umm-hmmm."

"Umm-hmmm-four." "Umm-hmmm-five." "Umm-hmmm-six."

Perhaps you're not certain you're speaking at the correct pitch level and tone focus. So let's use our back-up method to be sure the sound you are producing is correct.

THE INSTANT VOICE PRESS

Place one hand on your chest and your other hand on your stomach. Breathe in with your stomach moving out. Keep your lips closed, make a humming sound, and press in under the sternum in a quick staccato fashion. The sound escapes through the nose, but you will feel a buzz around the mouth and nose. The resonance you feel from the mask gives the well-used voice a clear and efficient sound.

Revert to this instant voice press during the learning stages whenever you seem unable to locate your correct pitch level.

GETTING YOUR VOICE GOING

Now say "umm-hmmm," using a rising inflection, with the lips closed.

And resume counting. "Umm-hmmm-seven." "Umm-hmmm-eight." "Umm-hmmm-nine."

Repeat the instant voice press.

Using this same pitch, repeat the following words:

"Hello."

"Really."

"Beautiful."

"Right."

"Ready."

"No."

"Go."

"Do."

These are energy words which naturally bring the voice forward, to the mask. But maybe you're not sure that you are making the transition from your old or habitual voice to your correct pitch level.

Standing, with legs straight, bend forward from the

waist as far as you can. Let your head and arms dangle loosely.

Say "Right!"
"Right-one."
"Right-two."
"Right-three."
"Right-four."
"Right-five."
"Right-really."
"No."
"Go."
"Hello."

Now stand straight up again, this time with your arms stretched high over your head.

Say "Hello!"
"Right."
"Really."
"Umm-hmmm."
"Umm-hmmm-my-umm-hmmm-name-umm-hmm-is" and add your own name here.

Lower your arms to your side and repeat the same:
"Hello!"
"Right."
"Really."
"Umm-hmmm."
"Umm-hmmm-my-umm-hmmm-name-umm-humm-is" and again add your own name here.

BREATHING FOR THE LIFE OF YOUR VOICE

Midsection breath support is crucial for the good health of your voice.

Lie on your back on the floor, with one hand on your chest and the other on your stomach. Breathe in *gently* through the nose. Exaggerated deep breathing is neither necessary nor desired. Your midsection or stomach moves outward as you breathe in, with the chest remaining still during inhalation. Now exhale through your mouth. As you do so, you will feel the midsection smoothly and slowly deflate.

Still lying on the floor, breathe in now through the mouth. Feel the midsection expand slightly. Exhale through the mouth. Breathing should be soft and easy, not forced or labored.

Repeat this exercise several times while still in the supine position, and then repeat the same sequence in the standing position. Keep one hand on the chest and the other on your stomach. Start by inhaling through the nose and exhaling through the mouth. Continue by inhaling *and* exhaling through the mouth. Be aware of your midsection expanding and deflating gently and smoothly.

Once you are comfortable with midsection breathing in the standing postion, proceed to a sitting position and repeat the sequence again. Remember to breathe gently. Deep breathing will tense the entire body and dry the throat.

Finally, keeping one hand on your midsection and the other on your chest, breathe in and say: "Umm-hmmm. Hello, right, really, my name is...." Feel the stomach move inward slightly as you speak. Take another gentle breath in, with the midsection expanding slightly, and say: "Hello. Beautiful. No. Go. Do."

Do not rush through these breathing exercises. Perform them at a leisurely pace. You might feel dizzy the first few times you do these exercises; this temporary phenomenon is caused by excessive oxygen intake. It should pass quickly.

RULES OF THE GAME

—If you have a recording device, make a tape of your old, habitual voice at the outset of the retraining process.

—Update your voice tape on occasion, often if you can. This way you can keep an accurate record of your progress, plateaus, and regressions.

—Be aware that your volume may sound louder to you than it really is in the initial stages. Your breath support in combination with correct pitch and tone focus has literally moved your sound to a different place.

—Allow time, if you can, in the morning to perform the simple exercises you have learned. Carry them out in the bathroom while you shower, shave, apply make-up, or blow-dry your hair. Resolve to "wake up" your sound and correctly place it—in the mask—every day.

—If you read the newspaper over breakfast, practice using your right, natural voice by reading aloud.

—As you drive to work, read aloud the names on the street signs as you make your way across town. Be aware of your pitch level, of tone focus, of breath support.

—Monitor your breath support during the day by discreetly placing one hand on your midsection when you speak. Check to see that your stomach moves out imperceptibly before you speak and gradually moves in as you use your voice.

—Talk *into* noise, not above it or below it. Your new voice should be clear and efficient without forcing it, in almost any situation.

—Assume a slower rate of speech in the initial phase of your retraining if necessary. Many readers will find this necessary in order to concentrate on the mechanics. After a period of familiarizing yourself with your new, right voice, you will no longer have to keep a slow pace.

Speed it up a bit, but not to the point where words or ideas run together.

—Ask a friend or relative to undergo voice retraining with you. You'll find that an associate or partner can make the process more fun, as well as more revealing.

—Play back your tape on occasion now. Compare and contrast the difference in your old, habitual sound and your new right sound.

—Practice reading aloud in the evening before you go to sleep. Again, monitor the various elements of correct voice production.

—Slowly become aware of your new sound concept. This is your special and unique sound. It is your right, natural voice, placed in the mask and buttressed with midsection breath support.

—Review the chapter on voice image. Ask yourself where your old voice image came from and what you got from it. Did it serve you well? Did it present you in your best possible light? Was it you? Is it still you?

—Decide that you wish to abandon your voice stereotype. No one wants to be a "type." You can be really good to yourself by accepting and embracing your individual and correct voice image.

NOW GO FOR THE MAGIC

The practical principles for correct voice production are now yours. You are well on your way toward achieving voice success through the use of your right, natural voice. Enjoy using it—because I know others will enjoy listening to it.

Audio and video cassettes of Dr. Cooper's successful techniques for voice improvement, including cures of spasmodic dysphonia, are now available. For information, phone (800) 932-3221. To contact Dr. Cooper, write to 11661 San Vicente Blvd., Suite 301, Los Angeles, CA 90049; Phone (310) 208-6047; Fax (310) 207-6769. Website: voice-doctor.com   E-mail: VOICEDOCTR@aol.com